BECOMING HISPANIC-SERVING INSTITUTIONS

REFORMING HIGHER EDUCATION:
INNOVATION AND THE PUBLIC GOOD
William G. Tierney and Laura W. Perna, SERIES EDITORS

BECOMING HISPANIC-SERVING INSTITUTIONS

Opportunities for Colleges and Universities

Gina Ann Garcia

JOHNS HOPKINS UNIVERSITY PRESS

Baltimore

Johns Hopkins University Press
2715 North Charles Street
Baltimore, Maryland 21218-4363
www.press.jhu.edu

Library of Congress Cataloging-in-Publication Data

Names: Garcia, Gina Ann, 1978– author.
Title: Becoming Hispanic-serving institutions : opportunities for colleges
    and universities / Gina Ann Garcia.
Description: Baltimore, Maryland : Johns Hopkins University Press, [2019] |
    Series: Reforming higher education : innovation and the public good |
    Includes bibliographical references and index.
Identifiers: LCCN 2018027533 | ISBN 9781421427379 (pbk. : alk. paper) |
    ISBN 1421427370 (pbk. : alk. paper) | ISBN 9781421427386 (electronic) |
    ISBN 1421427389 (electronic)
Subjects: LCSH: Hispanic Americans—Education (Higher) | Hispanic
    Americans—Education (Higher)—Case studies. | Hispanic American college
    students—Services for. | Hispanic American college students—Services
    for—Case studies. | Universities and colleges—United
    States—Administration. | Universities and colleges—United
    States—Administration—Case studies. | Educational equalization—United
    States. | Educational equalization—United States—Case studies.
Classification: LCC LC2670.6 .G35 2019 | DDC 378.1/982968073—dc23
LC record available at https://lccn.loc.gov/2018027533

A catalog record for this book is available from the British Library.

Special discounts are available for bulk purchases of this book. For more information, please contact Special Sales at 410-516-6936 or specialsales@press.jhu.edu.

Johns Hopkins University Press uses environmentally friendly book materials, including recycled text paper that is composed of at least 30 percent post-consumer waste, whenever possible.

To those students, faculty, staff, and administrators fighting the good fight, daily, within Hispanic-Serving Institutions

CONTENTS

Acknowledgments   ix

INTRODUCTION   What It Means to Serve Students   1

1   Creating the Dominant Narrative: The Racialization of
Postsecondary Institutions   7

2   White Institutions Becoming HSIs: The Case of Chicago   27

3   Enhancing the Cultural Experience of Latinx Students   47

4   Serving the Latinx Community in the Third Space   72

5   Pushing the Bar on Legitimized Outcomes   94

6   Reframing the HSI Narrative   115

Notes   139
References   141
Index   155

Fɪʀsᴛ ᴀɴᴅ foremost, I want to acknowledge the 106 participants in this study who spent time with me, shared their experiences with me, and trusted me with their stories. Thank you!

I acknowledge my family, including my life partner, Kenny Donaldson, and my children, Jovan Garcia Donaldson and Jaren Garcia Donaldson, for believing in me and for giving me the time and space to write this book. I love you all, and I can't imagine life without you. Thank you for being my biggest fans and for loving me unconditionally.

I had never thought about writing a book until the summer of 2016, as I began my two-year research leave supported by postdoctoral fellowships from the Ford Foundation and the Spencer Foundation/National Academy of Education. I cannot thank these foundations enough for supporting my development as a scholar. As a result of these fellowships, I had the time and creative space to dream up and write this book.

I would be remiss if I didn't acknowledge that my friend and colleague Dr. Rich Milner (Vanderbilt University) was the first person to plant the book-writing seed. During that summer in 2016, he told me that I should write a book, but he told me to wait until I got tenure. I didn't listen to that second piece of advice, but he made me believe that I could write a book. He provided feedback on the proposal and encouraged me the whole way through.

As the universe conspired, people kept coming into my life to convince me to write this book. After Rich, it was Dr. Bill Tierney at the University of Southern California (USC). While I was visiting USC during my Ford Foundation postdoctoral fellowship, I met with Dr. Tierney, and within the first ten minutes of our conversation he asked me if I wanted to write a book. I said "yes," not knowing that he was serious and would make it happen. But he was and he did. He told me about the higher education series that he edited through Johns Hopkins University Press. I am grateful to Dr. Tierney, along with Dr. Laura Perna at the University of Pennsylvania, his co-editor of the series, for giving me this opportunity. I also give thanks to Johns Hopkins University Press and Greg Britton for believing in this project and for making it happen.

I cannot thank Dr. Adrianna Kezar enough for her unconditional support in all of this. She was my mentor for the Ford Foundation postdoctoral fellowship. As a well-known, well-respected book author in the field of higher education, she was the perfect mentor in this process. She provided me with sample book proposals and encouraged me to develop the proposal while I was working with her through my fellowship. She edited the proposal and chapter 1, offering valuable suggestions and challenging me to write the dominant racial narrative for postsecondary institutions. She told me that I can't write counternarratives unless I first tell the master narrative. Chapter 1 was the most challenging and most rewarding chapter to write, because I had never conceptualized a master racial narrative for the postsecondary field. I am grateful to Dr. Kezar for being an inspiration and a mentor—and for pushing me to think outside the box.

One of the most essential scholar friends I have is Dr. Marc Johnston-Guerrero at Ohio State University. He was my BDBE (Best Dissertation Buddy Ever) at UCLA during our PhD program. He believed in me before I believed in myself. He told me that I was smart and had important things to say. He has since become my BSBE (Best Scholar Buddy Ever) and continues to read my work and provide valuable feedback. For this book, he read chapter 1 and chapter 6 and, like Dr. Kezar, pushed my thinking in whole new ways. As a race scholar, he was the best person to help me think through the racialization process for colleges and universities. Both chapters are better because of his feedback. I offer thanks to Dr. Johnston-Guerrero for being my friend and my intellectual superhero. You help me save the world through writing.

I am grateful to my colleague and friend Dr. Julie Posselt (USC), who helped motivate me to write this book. She wrote a book, *Inside Graduate Admissions* (Harvard University Press), as an untenured assistant professor and made me believe I could do it too. She also read my book proposal and offered words of encouragement throughout the process.

I also want to acknowledge Dr. Kris Gutiérrez (UC Berkeley), who was my mentor for my Spencer postdoc. She came into my life right when I needed a new way of thinking about chapter 4. I was terrified when I shared chapter 4 with her, but she was so encouraging and grace-ful and provided valuable feedback. I also want to thank my friend Dr. Letrell Crittenden (Philadelphia University + Thomas Jefferson University), a journalist by training who helped make chapter 4's coun-terstory more realistic.

This book would not have been possible without my team of graduate student researchers who helped me collect and analyze the data, including Lisanne Hudson, Jenesis Ramirez, Paulette Vincent-Ruz, Nikki Cristobal, Oscar Patrón, and Oscar Medina. I also want to acknowledge Emily Koren, who helped index the book.

Many other colleagues motivated and encouraged me at various stages of this book project. Some cheered me on from the sidelines, and some wrote with me so that I could get it done. I am grateful for my colleagues and friends at Pitt: Dr. Armando Garcia, Dr. Angie Cruz, Dr. Yodit Betru, Dr. Jaime Booth, Ms. Toya Jones, Dr. Elizabeth Rodriguez-Fielder, Ms. Matiangai Sirleaf, Dr. Sharon Ross, Dr. Linda DeAngelo, Dr. Lori Delale-O'Connor, and Dr. Kari Kokka. You were all so happy when I got the book contract. You celebrated me and my accomplish-ment. Thank you for loving and supporting me, always.

I also offer thanks to my UCLA advisor and mentor, Dr. Sylvia Hurtado, for teaching me how to be a scholar, writer, and thinker in higher education. My colleague and friend Dr. Anne-Marie Núñez helped me find my voice and my place within the literature on Hispanic-Serving Institutions. My HSI side sister, Dr. Marcela Cuellar, provided words of encouragement, challenged me, and helped me think differently about HSIs.

I am grateful to my friends and family, who have always cheered for me, not just in writing this book, but in life. I acknowledge my parents, Joe and Toni Garcia; my sister, Diane Garcia; my nieces and nephews, Karina, Mathew, Eliana, and Kaiden; my in-laws; my *tias* and *tios*, and all my cousins, for believing in me since I was a kid. I want to acknowl-edge my #FOCC2014 (Faculty of Color Cohort) family for being the best cohort ever and also the smartest group of overachievers I have ever met. I also acknowledge my best friend, Noime Penalba (Nono), for al-ways calling me the HSI Queen and for loving HSIs just because I do. I am grateful to all the friends who were in my life as I wrote this book, including Shonte Thomas, Nancy Armas, and Melissa Salazar.

BECOMING HISPANIC-SERVING INSTITUTIONS

What It Means to Serve Students

T HIS BOOK is about Hispanic-Serving Institutions (HSIs), which in the most technical sense are public and private, two- and four-year, not-for-profit, degree-granting, postsecondary institutions that enroll at least 25% full-time equivalent enrollment (FTE) Latinx undergraduate students.[1] These institutions are located in the United States, both on the mainland and in Puerto Rico, and represent a highly diverse set of institutions, ranging from broad access to more selective, associate-granting to doctoral institutions, and with varying organizational missions and purposes (Núñez & Elizondo, 2012). The only unifying characteristics of these institutions are that they enroll a significant number of Latinx students and they are nonprofit. The enrollment threshold is used to determine eligibility for federal designation as an HSI, yet not all postsecondary institutions that enroll 25% or more FTE Latinx undergraduate students are federally designated as such. With this book, I argue that an HSI organizational identity is more complex than a 25% enrollment threshold or a federal designation (Garcia, 2016, 2017). Both criteria are arbitrary, meaning that neither the percentage of Latinx students nor the federal designation actually defines what it means to be an HSI, or Latinx-serving.

While many recognize 1992 as the official "birth" of HSIs, others contend that the history of these institutions is much more storied, grounded in a long, steady battle fought by Latinx education advocates (Valdez, 2015). Valdez (2015) identifies 1979 as the year when the HSI seedling was planted, as members of eight social, political, and legal Latinx advocacy organizations formed the Hispanic Higher Education Coalition (HHEC; officially formed in 1978) and began delivering testimonies that stressed the need for increased funding for what they called "Hispanic Colleges" (i.e., colleges that enrolled a large percentage of Latinx students). Through their testimonies, members of the HHEC argued that although postsecondary institutions that enrolled a large percentage of Latinx students were eligible for Title III funding under the developing institutions definition, they had been inconsistently awarded funding through the competitive grant process (Valdez, 2015). Members of the HHEC continued to testify during major Higher Education Act (HEA) reauthorization periods, including 1981, 1984, and 1985 (Valdez, 2015).

Simultaneously, leaders at institutions that enrolled a large percentage of Latinx students formed a coalition that would raise awareness of the needs of their institutions (Santiago, 2006). The coalition became known as the Hispanic Association of Colleges and Universities (HACU), founded in 1986 in San Antonio, Texas, and it assumed much of the advocacy work for HSIs (MacDonald, Botti, & Clark, 2007; Santiago, 2006). HACU coined the term *Hispanic-Serving Institutions* at its first conference in 1986 (Santiago, 2006). In 1992, the HSI designation became official and the 25% enrollment level was solidified—important victories—but it wasn't until 1998 that the Developing Hispanic-Serving Institutions program was established under a separate section of the HEA known as Title V (Santiago, 2006). Since the formal recognition of HSIs, numerous scholars have published journal articles and books highlighting them, yet the debate continues about what it means, beyond the 25% and federal designation criteria, to serve Latinx students.

Need for This Book

The number of HSIs are increasing in the United States, which is connected to the surging enrollment of college students who self-identify as Latinx. In fall 2015, three million Latinx students enrolled in undergraduate programs in the United States, making up 17.6% of the total undergraduate population (National Center for Education Statistics,

2017). Of these Latinx students, 64% were enrolled in HSIs (Excelencia in Education, 2017c), making them significant sources of education for Latinx college students. According to Excelencia in Education (2017c), 472 institutions met the enrollment definition to be considered HSIs in fall 2015, representing 14% of institutions in the United States. Moreover, 323 institutions enrolled between 15% and 24% Latinx students, meaning they were emerging HSIs (Excelencia in Education, 2017a). These data suggest that HSIs are becoming more significant to the entire postsecondary landscape. As educators, administrators, and legislators, we cannot afford to ignore these rising giants.

With their increasing significance, the question remains: What does it mean, at an organizational level, to serve Latinx students? Even further, what does it mean to serve other racially minoritized, low-income, and first-generation students? While some suggest that graduating students is evidence of serving them, others say that HSIs must provide a culturally enhancing educational experience (Garcia, 2016, 2017). Either way, the presence and impact of HSIs cannot be denied within the larger population of postsecondary institutions. As HSIs become more important, there is a need to understand them as organizations *striving* to serve underserved populations.

I have argued that HSIs are redefining what it means to serve minoritized students (Garcia, 2016, 2017). With this book, I expand this argument, grounded in a racial analysis, highlighting how HSIs are undervalued as a result of being compared to white normative standards for postsecondary institutions. By *white normative standards*, I mean that all institutions of higher education are valued and gain status based on indicators of prestige and effectiveness that are grounded in whiteness. These indicators include SAT and ACT scores, selectivity, graduation rates, persistence rates, federal research dollars, and faculty publications (Astin, 2016). Yet, these measures have created a stratified system in which there are only a few elite institutions that are considered worthy of recognition, most of which are historically white. HSIs, which at the time of publication are mostly broad-access institutions (with a growing number of selective universities emerging or becoming HSIs), are generally situated at the lower levels of the collegiate hierarchy. Here I urge readers to consider the role of race within the hierarchy. As long as indicators of prestige and institutional effectiveness are grounded in whiteness, institutions that are racially minoritized (i.e., those that enroll large percentages of racially minoritized students) will continue to "underperform."

The purpose of this book is to counter the dominant racial narrative, which I define as the narrative centered on whiteness that is used in research and practice to evaluate postsecondary institutions. Using empirical data collected over two years at three HSIs in Chicago, Illinois, including institutional documents, historical archives, interviews, focus groups, participant observations, and photo elicitations, I use a counternarrative approach to highlight the ways that HSIs are reframing what it means to serve Latinx college students, while also questioning the extent to which they have been successful in doing this. Although I started this multi-site case study, called the Midwest HSI Study, by building off previous work (Garcia, 2013a, 2015, 2016, 2017; Garcia & Okhidoi, 2015) and asking the question, "How do organizational members make sense of an HSI identity?" the data revealed a much more complex story than I could tell in a single journal article. Although I recognize that HSIs are flawed (like all postsecondary institutions), this book highlights the value and uniqueness of each individual case examined. HSIs serve an important role in the larger landscape of postsecondary institutions; this book is an attempt to highlight this role. Further, as they continue to increase in number and impact, understanding them is becoming more important to a larger audience of educators, scholars, administrators, and legislators. Finally, this book lays out the challenges and opportunities in becoming an HSI.

Overview of the Book

In the first chapter, I lay out the dominant racial narrative of higher education, using a framework of racialization. I do this at an institutional level, giving examples of how the entire system of higher education is stratified by race. As a result of this stratification, institutions are valued based on the white dominant research and policy narrative for all postsecondary institutions. I highlight how the dominant narrative is based on white normative standards that disadvantage HSIs, which are racially minoritized as a result of enrolling large percentages of Latinx students (and other students of color). I also discuss how this has led to a deficit-based perspective that creates an unrealistic comparison of HSIs to white normative standards, including those connected to selectivity and prestige. In describing the dominant racial narrative, I set the foundation for the empirical chapters (chapters 3–5) in which I use a critical race counternarrative approach to tell the story of three HSIs in the Midwest.

In the second chapter, I provide an overview of the three four-year HSIs in the Midwest HSI Study, all of which have crossed the 25% Latinx enrollment threshold to be considered HSIs, meaning they are eligible for federal designation as HSIs. The level to which they have embraced their HSI status, however, varies tremendously. As such, I review the *Typology of HSI Organizational Identities* (Garcia, 2017), situating each within the typology. In presenting the institutions, I use quantitative data collected from the Integrated Postsecondary Educational Data System (IPEDS), providing a preliminary discussion on the extent to which these HSIs may be evaluated and criticized based on dominant white standards.

The third chapter is the first of three counterstories, focusing on the institution known in the Midwest HSI Study as Azul City University (ACU; a pseudonym). This institution is a four-year, midsize, public institution classified as a Master's College/University. The institution has been federally recognized as an HSI for more than twenty years and touts this designation on its website and in other media and official publications. Data from this site are robust and complicate the meaning behind being an HSI. As an institution that has long recognized its federal designation as an HSI, ACU has made intentional efforts to serve minoritized students, including Latinxs, low-income students, and undocumented immigrants. Yet it struggles to graduate them. Graduation is the most common white normative standard used to evaluate institutions of higher education and arguably the most important, meaning that all postsecondary institutions should strive to graduate students. As such, ACU recognizes its low graduation rate as a weakness. Without ignoring this fact, I lay out what it means for an institution to enhance the cultural and racial ways of knowing for Latinx college students, yet struggle to adequately graduate its students. This is what I call a Latinx-enhancing organizational identity (Garcia, 2017).

The fourth chapter highlights the institution known in the Midwest HSI Study as Amarillo Private College (APC; a pseudonym), which is a small private institution classified as an associate four-year college offering bachelor's and associate's degrees. The data reveal that the historical focus on the Latinx community makes APC unique in many ways. It offers an important counterstory, as it defies many of the normative practices among postsecondary institutions. I highlight how APC is providing educational advancement and outcomes for students while recognizing their racial and cultural ways of knowing, with a focus on language. As one of only a few institutions of higher education founded as bilingual, it has a rare place among postsecondary institutions. This institution is closely aligned with the HSI organizational identity type known as Latinx-serving (Garcia, 2017).

The fifth chapter focuses on the third institution in the Midwest HSI Study, Rosado Private University (RPU; a pseudonym). RPU is a small private institution classified as a master's college/university. It's also an urban, comprehensive university that provides a professional, career-focused undergraduate education by conferring associate's, bachelor's, and master's degrees. I lay out what it means to be an institution that graduates Latinx students in equitable numbers compared to white students, yet fails to enhance the cultural and racial ways of knowing of its students, or what I call a Latinx-producing organizational identity (Garcia, 2018b). This is also what I call "operating from a Latinx-neutral perspective" (Garcia, 2018b), which will be explored and complicated.[2]

The sixth and final chapter provides an approach for reframing HSIs in practice, research, and policy. Drawing from the three empirical chapters, I give examples of how HSIs have come to serve Latinx students in ways that are counter to the dominant narrative described in chapter one. I use the three sites as exemplars and provide valuable information on how institutions can provide an educational experience that enhances the racial and cultural ways of knowing of its students, while also contributing to their educational and career outcomes. I provide practitioners with strengths-based models and encourage policies and practices that will have a direct effect on the liberation of all people within HSIs (Garcia, 2018a). I also highlight the problems of conducting research with HSIs through a race-neutral lens, encouraging future organization-level research that centers race. I challenge researchers and legislators to recognize the value of HSIs and encourage future studies and policies that will do the same. The goal is to disrupt the dominant narrative about HSIs being "lesser than" non-HSIs, in hopes of finding more equitable ways of evaluating HSIs for their effectiveness and supporting them as they seek liberation for all.

ONE

Creating the Dominant Narrative

The Racialization of Postsecondary Institutions

THE FEDERAL recognition that Hispanic-Serving Institutions received in 1992 with the reauthorization of the Higher Education Act was a small victory for postsecondary institutions that enroll the largest percentage of Latinx college students. Recognizing the need to increase funding to these under-resourced institutions, advocates such as the Hispanic Higher Education Coalition and the Hispanic Association of Colleges and Universities knew that the most effective way to address the Latinx education gap, laid out very specifically in a report called *The Condition of Education for Hispanic Americans* (National Center for Education Statistics, 1980), was at the institutional level. The federal government's commitment to these institutions through formal recognition is symbolically and economically important, yet the Latinx education gap remains. Arguably, HSIs alone cannot sufficiently address the history of oppression and subjugation of Latinx students throughout the educational pipeline (Garcia, 2018a). Moreover, HSIs are expected to live up to a dominant white narrative that was created through a process of racialization.[1]

The racialization of postsecondary institutions in the United States is a process whereby colleges and universities are assigned value based on their institutional race (e.g., predominantly white, historically Black). Racialization is grounded in the idea "that race (and thus racial identities) is not an inherent category but rather is *made racial* through social interactions, positioning, and discourse" (Nasir, 2012, p. 5). It is a dynamic process, or what Moya and Markus (2010) call "a doing" (p. 21), where race is a set of actions that play out daily, with power and privilege assigned to people as a result of perceived racial characteristics. Essentially, racialization is a subjective process of "making up" racial categories based purely on ideological notions that are influenced by history, economics, culture, and politics (Omi & Winant, 2015, p. 105). Simultaneously, the racialization process leads to "othering," whereby some races are assigned value and others are diminished. While race and the process of racialization have mostly been theorized at an individual and group level, I describe the racialization of organizations, since postsecondary institutions have similarly been racialized. The process of racialization at the organizational level is intertwined with the individual, since the race of an institution has primarily been determined by the race of the students enrolled. However, here I argue that an institution's race is engrained in its organizational structures and reinforced by societal standards.

The practice of categorizing and assigning value based on race is historical and has varied across time and context (Omi & Winant, 2015). Racialization dates back to the founding of the United States, when white settlers established a society based on the denial and devaluing of the already-present indigenous people (Mills, 1997). Moya and Markus (2010) state that while the founders seemingly valued the indigenous people, as reflected in Thomas Jefferson's personal reflections on his admiration for them, they solidified a ranking system by race that justified unequal treatment under the laws and policies of the evolving country. This is no more evident than in the US Constitution, where slaves were considered three-fifths of a person and some Indians were excluded all together (Moya & Markus, 2010). With each political action that the white founders took throughout history, whiteness became engrained in culture, law, and society in the United States, not by accident, but through deliberate attempts to create a racial order (Mills, 1997). Whiteness, then, is conceptualized as a sociohistorical, structural ideology, rather than as a set of ideals about white people and their privileged identities. As Cabrera, Franklin, and Watson (2017) put it, "whiteness ≠ white people" (p. 18).

The racialization process, although intangible, has real implications, with whiteness reigning supreme in all aspects of society. As such, racial inequities become visible in areas such as education, health, law, housing, employment, sports, and the media (Moya & Markus, 2010). Educational inequities start at a very young age, with kids of color scoring lower on standardized tests and dropping out at higher rates than white kids do, not because of inherent racial differences, but because of unequal access to educational resources, skilled teachers, and high-quality curriculum (Darling-Hammond, 2010).[2] These inequities have been termed the "achievement gap," which refers to the disparities in standardized test scores between white kids and kids of color, yet this term fails to account for the long-term racialization that has deemed white kids as the norm and kids of color as deficient (Ladson-Billings, 2006; Milner, 2012). Instead, scholars have called for a focus on the "opportunity gap," arguing that many kids of color fall behind their white counterparts in education not because of innate differences, but because educators regularly draw from deficit frameworks, blame kids of color for mediocre performance, and rest on the myths of meritocracy, whereby they assume that people from all racial groups have equal access to opportunities for academic excellence (Milner, 2012). Racial inequities present across the educational pipeline are grounded in the racialization process of society, whereby educators and educational systems reinforce the racial hierarchy. For those kids of color who go on to postsecondary education, racial inequities become more pronounced, with students of color entering and graduating from postsecondary education at lower rates than white students (Aud, Fox, & Kewal-Ramani, 2010).

I move this argument from the individual to the organizational level, suggesting that racialization has affected postsecondary institutions, with colleges and universities being racialized through a historical set of actions that have privileged institutions enrolling white students (racially white) while subjugating those enrolling a large percentage of students of color (racially minoritized). Whiteness has become normalized in higher education through a series of ideological beliefs, including whiteness as color neutral ("we don't see race" or "anything but racism" arguments), whiteness as epistemological ignorance (racial ignorance is bliss), whiteness as ontological expansiveness (whiteness as physical space), whiteness as property (whiteness as a valuable commodity that cannot be transferred to racially minoritized people), and whiteness as racial comfort (enabling white people to feel safe and comfortable when it comes to race) (Cabrera et al., 2017). Moreover, whiteness has been normalized through a series of legislative actions and institutional polices. The racialization of postsecondary institutions can be traced back to the start of the higher education system in the United States, with whiteness engrained in the founding of Harvard (College) University. Even early attempts to include people of color were intended to rid them of their racial and cultural ways of knowing, as was the case with the establishment of Indian Schools in the colonial colleges (Wilder, 2013; Wright, 1991).

The racialization process was further solidified during the nineteenth century, with the establishment of Black colleges and universities before and after the Civil War. Early on, institutions such as Cheyney University, Wilberforce University, and Lincoln University were primarily established by white missionaries who feared that free Black people would become a menace to society if they were left uneducated (Gasman & Hilton, 2012). With the passing of the second Morrill Act in 1890, which mandated that any state that received federal funding must develop a state-supported land-grant institution as well as a "separate but equal" institution for Blacks, racial segregation at the postsecondary level was legitimized (Gasman & Hilton, 2012). Seventeen states complied with the act, adding to the growing list of Black colleges and universities (Thelin, 2011), including such institutions as Alcorn State University, Tuskegee University, and the University of Maryland Eastern Shore.

But as Omi and Winant (2015) remind us, the act of defining race has been "fraught with confusion, contradiction, and unintended consequences" (p. 105). As such, the separation of white and Black colleges had consequences, with history proving that separate was never equal. Many of the land-grant institutions established with the first Morrill Act of 1862 were racialized as white while evolving into highly regarded, well-resourced research universities, including the University of Wisconsin–Madison, Michigan State University, and Purdue University. In contrast, the land-grant institutions that were established in 1890 were racialized as Black and have struggled for equitable resources, funding, faculty, and infrastructures (Allen & Jewel, 2002; Brown, 1999; Harper, Patton, & Wooden, 2009). Some argue that the act intentionally segregated Black Americans, preventing them from gaining access to white institutions (Roebuck & Murty, 1993), while others contend that the federally supported vocational training model within the Black land-grant institutions relegated Blacks to an inferior position within society (Anderson, 1988). As such, Black institutions were racially minoritized and marked inferior and less desirable as a result of fewer resources, substandard facilities, and a subordinate vocational training model.[3] This mandated racial order remained in place, legally, until 1954, when institutions were forced to desegregate as a result of *Brown v. Board of Education of Topeka* (1954). Even then, a clear and equitable integration plan for postsecondary institutions was not defined.

The racial hierarchy of postsecondary institutions, which evolved as a result of the racialization process, has been well established. This means that despite efforts to become more compositionally diverse or inclusive of racially minoritized groups, whiteness continues to be valued, even at racially minoritized institutions such as HSIs and other Minority-Serving Institutions (MSIs). Through a number of interlocking elements, whiteness is validated within the curriculum and the classroom, with white knowledge and white ideologies passed on to all students, white and of color, with little resistance (Gusa, 2010). Furthermore, white voices, white histories, and white legacies are authenticated across campus, with little recognition of white dominance in policies, procedures, artifacts, and decision making (Gusa, 2010). As such, it no longer matters whether postsecondary institutions enroll a majority white population, as whiteness is recreated by individual actors within the institution and reinforced within the culture (Cabrera et al., 2017). There are numerous examples of this, yet the one most directly connected to HSIs is the fact that the curricular offerings at HSIs continue to be centered on whiteness, with a mere 2% of all courses at HSIs being centered on a racial/ethnic experience (Cole, 2011). The dominance of whiteness is detrimental when it comes to the hierarchical structure of the postsecondary educational system, with a few select institutions, racialized as white, considered "excellent," and others assumed to be less competent when it comes to effectively educating students, including those that are racially minoritized.

Racial Hierarchy of Postsecondary Education

The consequences of racialization are clear, with whiteness being normalized and privileged at the individual and organizational level, yet the racial hierarchy of postsecondary institutions is rarely discussed. Numerous scholars have highlighted that differentiation in institutional selectivity, mission, and resources contributes to the stratification of the postsecondary system, leading to inequitable access and outcomes for minoritized groups, including students of color and low-income students (Astin & Oseguera, 2004; Bastedo & Gumport, 2003; Posselt, Jaquette, Bielby, & Bastedo, 2012). Yet they fail to mention that the most selective, prestigious, and well-resourced institutions in the United States—those that graduate students who are most likely to go on to lucrative careers or graduate education—are typically racialized as white. Scholars critique those institutions for continuing to exclude minoritized students (an important critique) but give little attention to the system that values racially white institutions over racially minoritized institutions. In fact, scholars rarely discussed the race of the *institutions*, despite the fact that data suggest that the most selective colleges and universities enroll a much larger percentage of white students, meaning they continue to be white institutions (Carnevale & Strohl, 2013). So, while some scholars critique selective institutions for excluding racially minoritized students, there is no clear condemnation of the system that affirms and rewards institutions racialized as white. Moreover, there is complete disregard for those institutions that are racially minoritized, even though they provide access to students of color and other minoritized students (e.g., low income, immigrant), which is an important role within a stratified system.

Astin (2016), for example, condemns the stratification of the US postsecondary system and highlights the problems associated with the perpetual "pecking order," yet his criticism is race neutral, meaning he does not consider the role of race in contributing to the hierarchy. Astin (2016) posits that institutional excellence is determined by the number of "smart" students an institution has, the number of faculty superstars, and the amount of resources the institution has. Institutional quality and prestige, therefore, are determined by such indicators as SAT and ACT test scores of incoming students, the number of National Merit Scholars an institution enrolls, the number of faculty who publish extensively in peer-reviewed outlets, the amount of research dollars faculty members bring in, institutional endowment levels, extensive financial resources, and the number of academic programs offered (Astin, 2016).

Yet, Astin fails to note that standardized tests have historically discriminated against students of color, and he spends little time deconstructing the fact that white students outperform students of color in secondary education not because white students are smarter, but because structural inequities have led to racial inequities (Welner & Carter, 2013). Astin also fails to recognize the struggles of faculty of color in academe. Their scholarship continues to be undervalued, they continue to experience discrimination in the hiring and tenure process, and they are often tokenized and isolated within their institutions, which may lead to their attrition from the academy (Turner, González, & Wood, 2008). The measures that stratify the system, therefore, are inherently racialized, meaning they privilege white institutions and disadvantage racially minoritized institutions. The consequences of this process are that institutions that are racialized as white are valued, while those that are racially minoritized are subjugated.

This is apparent when observing that the US universities that consistently rank in the top ten, as determined by such entities as *U.S. News and World Report*, the *New York Times*, and *Times Higher Education*, are historically white institutions. These universities are Harvard, Yale, Princeton, Columbia, Stanford, Chicago, Massachusetts Institute of Technology (MIT), California Institute of Technology (Caltech), and Johns Hopkins University. While many of these institutions are becoming more diverse in their enrollment, with institutions like Stanford and MIT leading the list of the most diverse among *U.S. News and World Report's* top 100 universities in the United States, whiteness continues to be normalized through messages and practices embedded within these institution (Gusa, 2010).[4] Furthermore, racially minoritized institutions, including HSIs and other MSIs, are not found on the lists of top universities, suggesting that the racialization process has in fact reduced these institutions to a second-class status, while privileging white institutions.

The process of rating and ranking institutions reinforces the racial hierarchy within the US postsecondary educational system as a result of ranking categories that are grounded in white ideologies. Historically, institutional ranking dates back to the nineteenth century, when the US Bureau of Education began reporting statistical data about postsecondary institutions and professional associations, and accreditation bodies began publishing their own classifications (Stuart, 1995). Although the practice of ranking has changed forms over time, and despite criticism about the subjective nature of rankings, these lists continue to shape the public's perception of institutional reputation, quality, and excellence (Bastedo & Bowman, 2011; McDonough, Antonio, Walpole, & Perez, 1998; Stuart, 1995). Furthermore, they affect how institutions behave (Bastedo & Bowman, 2010; Institute for Higher Education Policy, 2009). One of the most well-known ranking publications, *U.S. News and World Report*, uses multiple indicators to determine "America's Best Colleges," including graduation and first-year retention rates, selectivity, financial resources, and alumni giving. It also asks administrators to assess its peers, and for national universities and national liberal arts colleges, it requests high school counselor ratings. The peer assessment aspect has been shown to reinforce the structural hierarchy of the system, as peers are more likely to see value in those institutions already perceived to be reputable and prestigious (Bastedo & Bowman, 2010).

Although the reliability and validity of the measures used to rank institutions have been questioned (McCormick & Zhao, 2005; McGuire, 1995), critics have failed to address the underlying racial discrimination of the ranking process. We know that the graduation and first-year retention rates of students of color are inequitable when compared to white students (Bensimon & Malcom, 2012). Institutions that strive to rank higher are therefore less likely to enroll students of color, simply because of the negative correlation between achievement and race. Standardized test scores mostly determine selectivity; thus, this measure is also influenced by race since it has already been noted that students of color perform at lower levels than white students do in this regard. The subjective nature of the peer assessment is also likely to be influenced by stereotypes about racial and ethnic groups that are entrenched in everyday life and contribute to the racialization process (Moya & Markus, 2010; Nasir, 2012). Moreover, because people of color are grossly underrepresented at the highest ranks of most universities, the selective group of deans and administrators who complete the peer assessment are likely to be white. Arguably, the ranking of institutions is ridden with methodological and reliability concerns that privilege a few institutions, most of which are racialized as white. Simultaneously, this process has real implications for racially minoritized institutions.

The Racialization of Hispanic-Serving Institutions

In 1992, with the reauthorization of the Higher Education Act, post-secondary institutions that had at least 25% FTE Latinx undergraduate students became known as Hispanic-Serving Institutions. Latinx political advocates and institutional administrators had fought a long, hard battle for recognition of institutions that enrolled a large percentage of Latinx students, starting in 1979 with testimonies by the HHEC during the HEA reauthorization hearings (Valdez, 2015). However, similar to when the federal government created the ethnic category "Hispanic" in 1973, also the result Latinx activists and legislators seeking recognition and legitimacy (Mora, 2014), the recognition of HSIs as an institutional type created a new racial category of "Brown" or "Latinized" institutions. Institutions that had been historically white were suddenly minoritized through legislative action. As with the federal government's attempts to "describe the world that exists by portraying a world that doesn't" with the creation of the ethnic category "Hispanic" (Rodriguez, 2002, p. 105), the racial category "Hispanic-Serving Institutions" is highly subjective and socially constructed. Moreover, the creation and federal recognition of both terms, *Hispanic* and *Hispanic-Serving Institutions*, ultimately has had consequences.

To be clear, people of Mexican, Latin American, Caribbean, and Spanish descent historically have been oppressed in the United States—educationally, economically, socially, and politically. But in creating a category that folded all of these groups into one (Hispanic), their minoritization became more tangible, as the health, education, economic, and political outcomes for this group could be highlighted, thus reifying the label "Hispanic" and reinforcing stereotypes and discrimination about this group. Although it is important to disaggregate outcomes by race and ethnicity in order to adequately address disparities, there are additional effects that must be noted; in this case, Latinx people were assigned a lesser value in US society. For example, the US Department of Health, Education, and Welfare developed a series of reports in the early 1980s, one of which, *The Condition of Education for Hispanic Americans*, showed great disparities in the educational outcomes of

Latinx people. With the dissemination of a national report that painted a picture of an entire racial/ethnic group in crisis, Latinxs were subjugated to a lower educational position in society. Latinxs who excel academically are seen as the exception, as the narrative about Latinxs being undereducated was solidified.

Similarly, in creating a designation for institutions that enroll large percentages of Latinx students, HSIs fell in place within a racial order that privileged institutions racialized as white. To be clear, HSIs were already under-funded, under-resourced, and under-valued when they gained recognition. The federal designation increased scrutiny, with little regard for the racialized nature of the system. This has led to criticism, with some scholars calling HSIs *Hispanic-enrolling*, a term that has become derogatory in nature by suggesting that simply enrolling a large percentage of Latinxs without graduating them is egregious and ineffective. While these scholars originally intended to call on HSIs to graduate Latinx students in equitable numbers, the term *Hispanic-enrolling* is now seen as negative. HSIs are also criticized for operating like white institutions, meaning they teach a white curriculum, employ white faculty and administrators, and foster racism and discrimination in similar ways as racially white institutions. Yet these criticisms are inherently tied to a system that values all things white. As such, critics may actually be arguing that HSIs are not serving Latinx students *because they are not white institutions.*[5]

Within the hierarchy of institutions, HSIs are relegated to second-class status because they are compared to white normative standards. Of the 435 institutions that had reached the enrollment threshold of 25% Latinx students in fall 2014, few were highly selective institutions or research institutions, and *U.S. News and World Report* did not consider any as among "the best." In fact, many HSIs are broad-access institutions with high acceptance rates, and many are open access institutions, meaning they enroll students regardless of academic merit or test scores (Núñez & Bowers, 2011; Santiago, 2006). They also have fewer resources than other institutions, spend less per FTE, and enroll low-income students, who are more likely to receive Pell Grants and less likely to take out loans (Cunningham, Park, & Engle, 2014; Núñez & Elizondo, 2015), all of which are markers of a subordinated status within the hierarchy of postsecondary institutions. Furthermore, many

HSIs offer a limited number of degree programs (Núñez & Elizondo, 2012), which is also indicative of a subjugated status.

Whether HSIs, and other racially minoritized institutions, are inferior is debatable, mostly because the indicators of excellence and greatness are subjective. The reality is that these indicators are based on research and policy narratives that are grounded in whiteness and white ways of knowing. As such, racially minoritized institutions are evaluated in comparison to white institutions. The scholarly and policy debates about HSIs continue to be focused on whether they are actually *serving* Latinx and other minoritized students. Beyond the enrollment requirement, there is no federally mandated expectation about processes or outcomes at HSIs. This has created a debate about measuring the effectiveness and viability of HSIs.

Some scholars suggest that academic outcomes are the best indicators of effectively serving Latinx students (Contreras & Contreras, 2015; Contreras, Malcom, & Bensimon, 2008; Flores & Park, 2013, 2015; Garcia, 2013b; Rodríguez & Calderón Galdeano, 2015). These indicators include graduation and persistence rates, time to degree, and transfer rates from community colleges to four-year institutions. Others argue that nonacademic outcomes, such as academic self-efficacy and student engagement, could be important indicators of how well HSIs are serving Latinx students (Cuellar, 2014; Fosnacht & Nailos, 2015; Garcia, Patrón, Ramirez, & Hudson, 2018; R. G. González, 2008). Some also believe that providing a positive, culturally engaging campus that values students' ways of knowing is essential to effectively serving Latinx students at HSIs, and that creating this campus environment will ultimately lead to other outcomes (Arbelo-Marrero & Milacci, 2016; Espinoza & Espinoza, 2012; Garcia & Okhidoi, 2015; Garcia & Ramirez, 2018; Kiasatpour & Lasley, 2008; Maestas, Vaquera, & Muñoz Zehr, 2007; Núñez, Murakami-Ramalho, & Cuero, 2010).

These measures of effectiveness, however, are based on white normative standards that have been influenced by the racialization process. Beyond the legislative actions and arbitrary ranking system that have established a racial order of postsecondary institutions, a majority of the empirical research and policies on institutions of higher education has been conducted, validated, and normalized by white people studying white students at white institutions. Stevens (2015) reminds us that academically selective institutions have received "the lion's share of academic and media attention" (p. 2); I extend this argument to suggest that those academically elite institutions have also been racially white institutions. The empirical research that is the foundation of the academic field of higher education has produced a dominant research narrative that is based on whiteness and has essentially determined that "the best" institutions are white institutions.

Racialized Knowledge and White Dominant Narratives

Historically, research on white institutions solidified a white dominant narrative, one that is reinforced in contemporary research, shapes how scholars think and write about postsecondary education, and ultimately influences policy. White research, or what Bonilla-Silva and Zuberi (2008) call "white logic," "refers to a context in which white supremacy has defined the techniques and processes of reasoning about social facts" (p. 17). Bonilla-Silva and Zuberi (2008) remind us that social science was developed alongside a racially stratified system, thus deeming research grounded in white ideologies legitimate, objective, and socially acceptable. Within education research, the racialization process has produced a long history of empirical evidence that suggests that people of color are academically inferior to white people, with little recognition of the sociohistorical contexts that have produced these results (Allen, Suh, González, & Yang, 2008). At the same time, research has racialized postsecondary institutions as white institutions, simultaneously deeming white institutions as superior, and privileging white narratives. Racially minoritized institutions have been silenced in research because of their subjugated position. Reviewing foundational literature in the field of higher education provides evidence of this.

The foundational research in the field of higher education dates back to the 1960s. In an effort to better understand the body of knowledge that was shaping the field at the time, I first reviewed the work of Weidman, Nelson, and Radzyminski (1984), who surveyed members of the Association for the Study of Higher Education (ASHE) in the 1980s and asked them to list the books they considered "basic reading" in their courses. The most commonly listed book was Clark Kerr's 1963 book, *The Uses of the University*. Kerr wrote this book in the early 1960s, describing the evolution of the university into what he called the "multiversity." While Kerr's ideas and predictions about the evolution of postsecondary institutions continue to be relevant today, his analysis was based on his experience as chancellor of a then predominantly white institution, the University of California, Berkeley.

Also at the top of Weidman et al.'s (1984) list was Laurence Veysey's 1965 book, *The Emergence of the American University*. This book is regarded as a foundational history book for those who study higher education in the United States. Veysey documented the historical development of the institutions that would became some of the most elite institutions in the country, including Harvard, Yale, Columbia, Princeton, the University of Chicago, Johns Hopkins University, and Stanford. While Veysey's arguments about the structure, atmosphere, goals, and overall characteristics of the research university are accurate for the top twenty elite institutions in this country, they fail to account for the remaining 4,000 institutions that do not function like the elites and whose primary purpose is not research. While HSIs were not yet established in the time period that Veysey wrote about (1865–1910), Historically Black Colleges and Universities (HBCUs) were. Yet, he did not include these institutions, essentially silencing Black voices and giving precedence to whiteness and white institutions.

The third most cited work was Frederick Rudolph's 1962 book, *The American College and University: A History* (Weidman et al., 1984). Like Veysey, Rudolph gave a rich historical account of postsecondary institutions, but Rudolph focused a majority of his attention on the nineteenth and early twentieth centuries and highlighted a more traditional college experience at more traditional institutions. Even today, this text continues to be relevant within courses focused on the history of higher education, especially since Rudolph gave attention to co-curricular experiences and intercollegiate football, which few other history books have done. Yet Rudolph dedicated minimal space to community colleges and HBCUs, essentially silencing Black people and the institutions they were relegated to. As depicted by Veysey and Rudolph, the development and expansion of the system of higher education in the United States was largely a white process for white people in white institutions.

Other texts, beyond those cited by Weidman and colleagues, are also regarded as foundational readings for scholars who study higher education. Burton Clark's 1970 book, *The Distinctive College*, has remained relevant for more than forty years. Clark highlighted the factors that make liberal arts colleges great by focusing on three elite colleges: Antioch, Reed, and Swarthmore. His argument was that many postsecondary institutions suffer from mediocrity, while few strive for greatness. By providing in-depth, historical accounts of three institutions that Clark argued had reputations for being high quality, he suggested that others could learn how to be successful and effective. He described Antioch's evolution to greatness, Reed's revolutionary push toward greatness, and Swarthmore's birth into greatness (Clark, 1970). With each account, he described charismatic leaders and the deep cultural values necessary for becoming distinctly excellent. In painting a picture of greatness, Clark focused on three white institutions, thus solidifying whiteness as great.

While some books established whiteness as normal through their historical accounts of the emergence of US postsecondary education system, others were more critical of the system, highlighting its inevitable stratification. Christopher Jencks and David Riesman, in their 1968 book, *The Academic Revolution*, provided a sociological perspective of American higher education. With this foundational book, the authors argued that the stratification seen in society is essentially maintained through postsecondary education. While their account was critical and highlighted the ways in which elite colleges have come to serve the upper middle class by preventing the lower working class from entering, their argument was largely based on social class, with less attention paid to race. In detailing the roles and functions of various types of colleges, including women's colleges, Protestant colleges, Catholic colleges, and "Negro" colleges, they introduced various perspectives on gender, religion, and race, yet like many other sociological texts, the underlying argument is class based. Although sufficiently critical, the foundational higher education texts written by sociologists also reinforced whiteness as normal.

Employing an analysis grounded in the theory of population ecology and based on a sample of institutions in eight states, Robert Birnbaum, in his 1983 book, *Maintaining Diversity in Higher Education*, argued for the value of institutional diversity. He measured institutional diversity through institutional control (public vs. private), size, degree levels offered, sex of the students, and "minority" enrollment (Birnbaum, 1983). Like Jencks and Riesman, Birnbaum attempted to include race as a category for defining institutional diversity, but his analysis fell short, as he admits that "there were no institutions that in 1960 enrolled a majority nonwhite students who were not black" (Birnbaum, 1983, p. 93). With his empirical evidence being based on institutional data from 1960 and 1980, a time when institutions of higher education mostly enrolled white people, his argument is largely framed from a white perspective, with less attention paid to institutional racial diversity as an important type of institutional diversity.

As leading white scholars laid the foundation for the field of higher education, they based their arguments on knowledge of white people in white institutions, as expected, considering the historical, legal, educational, and economic constraints and exclusions at the time. This is not to discount foundational knowledge on institutions of higher education and the people within them or the scholars who did the important work of establishing the field of higher education. It is just to note the historical significance of normalizing whiteness in postsecondary research. This is also not to discount the work of scholars who have given voice to minoritized people and racially minoritized institutions. Craig Steven Wilder's 2013 book, *Ebony and Ivy: Race, Slavery, and the Troubled History of America's Universities*, provided a much-needed revisionist historical account of the colonial colleges, offering details about the role of the Trans-Atlantic slave trade and settler colonialism in the development of such institutions as Harvard, Yale, and Princeton. Similarly, Marybeth Gasman and Roger Geiger edited a book in 2012 called *Higher Education for African Americans before the Civil Rights Era, 1900–1964*, which featured chapters from some of the most prolific historians of Black higher education and highlighted the experience of Black folks in racially minoritized institutions of higher education.

Yet it is hard not to notice the fifty-one-year lag time between the publication of Rudolph's classic book, *The American College and University: A History*, and Wilder's revisionist account of higher education, reinforcing my point that knowledge of institutions of higher education has historically been white, thus solidifying whiteness as the foundation of our ways of knowing. Racialized knowledge and white ways of knowing are continually transferred from faculty, white and of color, to students of higher education, who go on to be the leaders of US postsecondary institutions, policy advocates in Washington, DC, and future scholars of higher education who transmit white knowledge into white practice and white policies.

Whiteness transcends from research into policy, thus reinforcing racial order. Although some would like to believe that education policy is race neutral, a critical race view of policy suggests that it is "not a mechanism that delivers progressively greater degrees of equity, but a process that is shaped by the interests of the dominant white population" (Gillborn, 2014, p. 28). A striking example is the passing of Arizona's infamous House Bill 2281, which banned ethnic studies classes in the state, despite the fact that evidence showed that students who took classes through the Mexican American Studies Department in the Tucson Unified School District outperformed all other students in the state on standardized tests and matriculated into college at a high rate (Cabrera, Milem, Jaquette, & Marx, 2014). A program that was effectively decreasing the opportunity gap between white students and students of color was seen as a threat to white supremacy, which led to the enactment of a policy that would maintain racial order (i.e., continue to privilege white students over students of color). Another example is seen in Texas, where a critical race analysis of the school funding model revealed that it systematically disadvantages majority Mexican American school districts, as evidenced in inequitable allocations of operational, maintenance, and facilities funding (Alemán Jr., 2007). An inequitable funding model contributes to the opportunity gap and reinforces a racialized educational system.

At the postsecondary level, policies and legislative actions have maintained white supremacy while reinforcing racial order. After more than fifty years of a racially segregated educational system as a result of *Plessy v. Ferguson*, the 1954 ruling of *Brown v. Board of Education of Topeka* overturned the separate but equal doctrine (Brown, 1999). But the focus of this policy was on primary and secondary schooling, with less attention paid to colleges and universities until 1964 with the passing of the Civil Rights Act (Brown, 1999). Since 1964, there have been lengthy legal battles in nineteen states to desegregate discriminatory dual systems of higher education that reinforced a racial hierarchy, with white flagship institutions prevailing and Black colleges struggling (Brown, 1999; Gasman & Hilton, 2012). Language calling for "race-neutral policies" and "good-faith efforts" in such cases as *United States v. Fordice* (1992) is highly subjective and has failed to eliminate the postsecondary racial hierarchy. Admission policies continue to maintain racial order through arbitrary policies, such as a minimum ACT score required for admission, that discriminate against Black students who seek entrance into elite white institutions (Gasman & Hilton, 2012). Desegregating postsecondary institutions within a racialized system that values white institutions while subjugating racially minoritized institutions inevitably will be a long legal and political struggle.

The passage of the Civil Rights Act of 1964 led to a mandate for postsecondary institutions to take affirmative action to address the racial inequities created by years of government-enforced segregation and legislative action (Garces, 2015). Many of the resulting efforts involved changes to admission policies and were primarily undertaken by the white public flagship institutions that had long histories of discriminating against people of color. Despite the seemingly good-faith efforts of these institutions to remedy racial discrimination, the adoption of race-conscious admission policies in the 1960s and 1970s ultimately led to a long battle over the legality of these policies, from *Regents of the University of California v. Bakke* in 1978 to *Fisher v. University of Texas* in 2013 (Garces, 2015). Although the ruling in *Fisher* maintains that racial diversity is a compelling educational interest—meaning it is beneficial for white people and white institutions—the attack on race-conscious admission policies has negatively affected the enrollment of students of color in some flagship state institutions, including those in California (Contreras, 2005), thus reinforcing white racial dominance in postsecondary education.

Beyond legislative actions, the "new accountability movement," which focuses on inputs, progress, and overall outcomes over state governance structures (Jones, Jones, Elliott, Russel Owens, Assalone, & Gándara, 2017; McLendon, Hearn, & Deaton, 2006), has also contributed to the maintenance of a racial hierarchy. While higher education accountability conversations have focused on access, affordability, and outcomes, institutions are rarely able to perform well in all three areas (Rodríguez & Kelly, 2014). As such, institutions will likely sacrifice one for another (usually access for outcomes). Racially minoritized institutions that are committed to increasing access to students of color (who also happen to have the highest need) simultaneously decrease the most commonly measured outcome: six-year graduation. A focus on accountability, therefore, reinforces the racial hierarchy, with racially minoritized institutions seemingly underperforming with regard to outcomes when compared to white institutions. There is often little regard for the characteristics of incoming students at racially minoritized institutions—mainly that they are also more likely to be low income—and the effect that these characteristics have on six-year graduation rates (Núñez, 2014). Moreover, the accountability movement has also led to the controversial idea of developing a ratings system that can be tied to federal funding (Espinosa, Crandall, & Tukibayeva, 2014). Performance funding may have unintended consequences, such as admitting fewer underprepared students (who may also be students of color) and changing the mission of the institution (which may be to provide access) (Dougherty & Reddy, 2013), further racializing the system.

Are HSIs Reinforcing or Challenging the White Dominant Narrative?

As postsecondary institutions in the United States evolved within a racialized society, they were simultaneously racialized, or made racial, through deliberate actions and policies. It is clear that racial meanings have historically been attached to colleges and universities, similar to the ways in which they have been attributed to people, primarily influenced by social, political and economic developments (Obasogie, 2013). This is evident in the research and policy narratives for postsecondary institutions, which I have described as centered on whiteness. As such, postsecondary institutions are evaluated based on white research (i.e., research centered on white people and white institutions) and white normative standards.

Racially minoritized institutions, including HSIs, are undervalued as a result of being compared to these standards. Rather than appreciating that these institutions increase access for a large percentage of students of color, who may also be low income, first-generation college students, immigrants, and post-traditional students (i.e., older, part-time, commuter; Santiago, 2013), they are penalized because, as Astin (2016) argues, they do not enroll the "smartest" students, employ the "most talented" faculty, offer an extensive array of degree programs, or have the same level of resources as white institutions. As subjective as these measures are, they reinforce the racially stratified system that values a few white elite institutions and relegate numerous racially minoritized institutions to the lower levels of the hierarchy. While scholars agree that the postsecondary system is stratified, few have looked at this process through the lens of racialization. The racialization process has real implications for institutions that are deemed less worthy, less valuable, and less effective. This has led to a deficit-based perspective of HSIs.

As the number of HSIs in the United States increases, there is a need to more closely examine these institutions, both at the micro and macro levels. In fall 2015, 472 institutions were eligible for the HSI designation, which represents 14% of all postsecondary institutions in the United States (Excelencia in Education, 2017c). There were also 323 emerging HSIs (eHSIs), or those that enroll 15%–24% Latinx students (Excelencia in Education, 2017a). The large number of eHSIs indicates that the number of HSIs will continue to grow in the coming years, which is reason to assess their significance within the system. HSIs now enroll 64% of all Latinx college students (Excelencia in Education, 2017c), as well as a large percentage of other students of color (e.g., Black and Asian students), low-income students, first-generation college students, and immigrant students (Malcom-Piqueux & Lee Jr., 2011; Núñez & Bowers, 2011). They also confer 60% of all associate's degrees to Latinx college students and 40% of all bachelor's degrees to this group (Malcom-Piqueux & Lee Jr., 2011), and graduate 40% of all STEM (science, technology, engineering, and math) bachelor's degrees (Harmon, 2012), meaning they are contributing to the STEM workforce.

In this chapter, I described the dominant white research and policy narrative in order to make sense of how the HSIs I discuss in the remaining chapters reinforce the racial order of postsecondary institutions. While white research and white policies legitimate institutions of higher education, they also reify a system that considers white colleges to be good and racially minoritized institutions to be less desirable. The false perception that HSIs are less effective when it comes to serving minoritized students lacks a solid objective grounding and has little to do with their actual value within the larger system of postsecondary education. In using a critical race methodology, I account for the racialization process and the role it plays in framing HSIs in research and policy rhetoric. Furthermore, this approach allows me to challenge the white ideological notions that subjugate HSIs to the lower levels of a racially stratified system.

I use a critical race methodology known as counterstorytelling (Solórzano & Yosso, 2002) to disrupt the white narrative that has relegated HSIs to second-class status. The three counterstories I present are based on empirical data from a multiple case study of four-year HSIs in Chicago, Illinois (The Midwest HSI Study). In developing the counterstories, I drew from the lived experiences of faculty, staff, and students within three HSIs. I constructed composite counterstories using various data sources, including one-on-one interviews with participants, focus groups interviews with students, secondary data from IPEDS, existing literature on HSIs, ethnographic observations, and document reviews. As suggested by Solórzano and Yosso (2002), the composite counterstories are also grounded in theoretical notions about what it means to become an HSI. Based on my own theoretical framework of four HSI organizational identities, I highlight what it looks like to be Latinx-enhancing, Latinx-producing, and Latinx-serving (Garcia, 2017). The counterstory composites are factual and grounded in empirical data, yet conveyed as fictional scenarios (Solórzano & Yosso, 2002).

Although I originally sought to demonstrate the value of racially minoritized institutions, such as HSIs, using a counterstory approach, I realized that while these institutions provide great value to the students they serve and the system as whole, they maintain the racial order of the system. Therefore, throughout the book, I question whether HSIs are reinforcing the dominant white narrative or challenging it, noting the inevitable tensions that these institutions face within a racially ordered system.

White Institutions Becoming HSIs

The Case of Chicago

R ACIALLY WHITE institutions in the United States are becoming Hispanic-Serving Institutions at a rapid rate as a result of the surging enrollment of college students who self-identify as Latinx. Colleges and universities located in geographic areas that have large Latinx populations are becoming HSIs at much higher rates than those institutions located in regions with fewer Latinx people. The Midwest is one such region, with Illinois alone accounting for a majority of the growth in the Latinx population in this region. In fact, Illinois is one of five states with the largest Latinx populations (2.2 million) (Stepler & Lopez, 2016). Even further, a majority of Latinxs in Illinois live in Chicagoland.

The number of HSIs in the Midwest reflects the Latinx population in this area. In fall 2014, there were twenty-three institutions in the Midwest that were eligible for federal designation as HSIs. This included seventeen institutions in Illinois, one in Indiana, four in Kansas, and one in Ohio (Excelencia in Education, 2016b). There were also thirty-four emerging HSIs in the Midwest: twenty-three in Illinois, two in Indiana, three in Kansas, one in Missouri, four in Nebraska, and one in Wisconsin (Excelencia in Education, 2016a). While the Southwest, the Northeast, and Puerto Rico have larger densities of HSIs and eHSIs, the emergence of these institutions in the Midwest is notable, especially when considering the growth of the Latinx population in this region (Brown & Lopez, 2013). As enrollment-driven institutions, the number of HSIs will continue to increase as the Latinx population grows, making the Midwest a prime area to study the evolution of these racially minoritized institutions.

Typology of HSI Organizational Identities

The most salient question that administrators working at HSIs, scholars studying HSIs, and legislators advocating for HSIs are asking is, "What does it mean for a college or university to serve Latinx college students?" Arguing that this is an identity question, I developed the *Typology of HSI Organizational Identities* (see figure 1) based on a social constructionist perspective of identity development. Before drawing on empirical data, I grounded the typology in the extant literature on HSIs and incorporated two social constructionist theories used by sociologists of organizations (institutional theory) and organizational behaviorists (cultural theory).

Institutional Theory

Within the scholarship on organizations, institutional theory can be classified as an environmental theory (Bess & Dee, 2008). In many ways this theory is deterministic, assuming that organizations act according to environmental regulations and changes, and in accordance with other organizations within the same population. Institutional theory is appropriate for studying the evolution of HSIs and the identity construction process because the HSI designation is federally constructed and enrollment of Latinxs is affected by state and federal legislation such as affirmative action and financial aid regulations (Garcia, 2015). Moreover, HSIs tend to fall into a process of mimicry, looking to the field for models of how to be Latinx-serving, as expected in an environment fraught with uncertainty (Meyer & Rowan, 1977).

Contemporary institutional theory is inclusive of three main pillars, including regulative, normative, and cognitive elements (Scott, 1995). Drawing on institutional theory for the study of HSIs, therefore, I assume that HSIs make meaning of their environments and engage in activities that are considered legitimate within their field based on regulatory, normative, and cognitive pressures (Scott, 1995; Suddaby, 2010). Moreover,

I presume that HSIs adopt behaviors that conform with symbolic, normative expectations of the environment, rather than making decisions that fulfill rational, economic goals (Meyer & Rowan, 1977; Suddaby, 2010). HSIs ultimately seek legitimacy by conforming to external pressures within the field of higher education, modeling similar organizations based on mimetic processes, and adopting normative standards set by professional organizations (DiMaggio & Powell, 1983).

From an institutional perceptive, an organizational identity is constructed based on an organizational reference to others within the field, or what Whetten and Mackey (2002) call a "self-referent." As institutions seek legitimacy within a given field, organizational members construct their identity based on a desire to be like other organizations. In the case of postsecondary institutions, oftentimes colleges and universities want to be like their aspirational peers, or those that are performing well, based on normative measures. For HSIs, this is no different, as organizational members are likely to construct an HSI organizational identity based on what they know about other HSIs or other postsecondary institutions in general. As I argue in chapter 1, postsecondary institutions are racialized, with racially white institutions being valued and normalized, and racially minoritized institutions being subjugated. Thus, members are likely to construct an HSI organizational identity in relation to white normative standards.

Cultural Theory

The theory of organizational culture is extensive, spanning multiple disciplines, from anthropology to organizational behavior (Bess & Dee, 2008). Scholars have been drawn to cultural theories in the study of postsecondary education, often as a way to diagnose management and administrative problems within colleges and universities (Tierney, 1988). Yet there is little agreement about the definition and operationalization of culture within research (Martin, 2002). One common definition is that culture is "shared," suggesting that people across the organization have a collective meaning about the history, beliefs, values, symbols, norms, and rituals of the organization. Martin (2002) reminds us, however, that conflict and disagreement about cultural ideations and material manifestations are also important, particularly as power and social identities come into play. In studying HSIs through a cultural lens, this is an important element to consider, as perceptions of culture are likely to be fragmented, with people lacking consensus (Martin, 2002) as a result of their own social identities and positions within the organization.

There is also a disagreement about whether culture is a variable, used to predict specific outcomes within organizations, or a metaphor, used as a symbolic lens for understanding life within an organization (Smircich, 1983). In the study of HSIs, scholars have mostly used culture as a variable, arguing that HSIs provide a place where Latinx students can feel linguistically, culturally, and racially connected to peers, faculty, and administrators, and suggesting that this unique culture will lead to desirable outcomes, such as sense of belonging, persistence, and graduation (Garcia, 2015). This conceptualization of culture as a variable is largely connected to research on campus climate, which suggests that a positive or welcoming climate will lead to greater outcomes for minoritized students (Hurtado, Alvarez, Guillermo-Wann, Cuellar, & Arellano, 2012).

From a cultural perspective, organizational identity is constructed based on members' perceptions of the organizational elements that set them apart from other organizations, rather than focusing on those that make them similar (as in institutional theory). Moreover, they conceptualize their identity based on tacit and symbolic assumptions about the values and beliefs that transcend the organization (Garcia, 2017). Members trying to make sense of an HSI organizational identity often draw on the unique ways in which HSIs create a positive campus climate for Latinxs, engage with the Latinx community, support Latinx students through culturally relevant practices, and enhance Latinx students' racial/ethnic identity development (Garcia, 2017; Garcia & Okhidoi, 2015; Garcia et al., 2018).

Combining Perspectives

Guided by institutional theory and cultural theory, I agree strongly with Pedersen and Dobbin (2006), who state, "The antinomy between the central findings of neoinstitutional and organizational culture theories, we argue, reflects a wider social process in which organizations create legitimacy by adopting recognizable forms and create identity by touting their uniqueness" (p. 898). Theorists from both camps argue that an organizational identity is grounded in a "collective meaning structure," but institutionalists believe the meaning making happens at the field level among groups of organizations, while culturalists believe it occurs within the organization among individuals (Pedersen & Dobbin, 2006, p. 899). Guided by these principles, I developed the *Typology of HSI Organizational Identities*, grounded in empirical data from an in-depth case study of a four-year HSI in the Southwest. I proposed the typology, inclusive of four quadrants, based on how organizational members in the study constructed an *ideal* HSI identity drawing on both institutional ways of knowing and aspects of their unique culture. The overwhelming majority of participants said that an HSI should produce desirable outcomes typically used to measure institutional success with regard to serving students (e.g., graduation rates). Others suggested that an HSI should enact a culture that enhances the racial/ethnic experiences of Latinx students. Combining these seemingly unique indicators of an identity for serving Latinxs, I argue that both outcomes and culture are essential to an HSI's organizational identity (Garcia, 2017).

When members construct their organizational identity as *Latinx-enrolling*, they suggest that although their institution enrolls the minimum 25% Latinx students needed to become federally designated as an HSI, it does not produce equitable outcomes for Latinx students and does not have an organizational culture that enhances or supports the development of Latinx students. A second organizational identity, *Latinx-producing*, is constructed by members who suggest their institution enrolls at least 25% Latinx students and produces positive outcomes for Latinx students. Members may say that the institution is effective in graduating students or training students for future careers

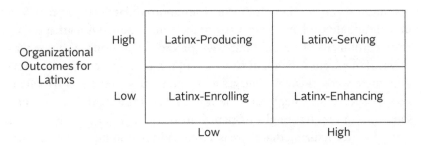

Figure 1. Typology of Hispanic-Serving Institution Organizational Identities. Garcia (2017b).

and graduate school. Members may not recognize, however, that the institution lacks the culture for supporting the success and development of Latinx students.

A third organizational identity that members may construct is a *Latinx-enhancing* identity, which is based on enrolling a minimum 25% Latinx students and enacting a culture that enhances the racial/ethnic experience of Latinx students. Members make sense of their HSI organizational identity in this way when they draw on deeply embedded cultural practices and norms that are grounded in Latinx ways of knowing and being, yet also recognize that the institution does not produce an equitable number of outcomes for Latinx students. A fourth identity, a *Latinx-serving* organizational identity, is constructed by members who know that the institution enrolls 25% Latinx students, produces an equitable number of outcomes for Latinx students, and enacts a culture that enhances the educational and racial/ethnic experience of Latinx students. Intentionally, the typology is not stage-based, and there are no specific rankings of the four HSI organizational identity types. Instead, I contend that all types of HSIs are worthy and valid within a racially stratified system of higher education.

The Midwest HSI Study

In order to observe the process of white institutions becoming HSIs, I turned to one subpopulation of HSIs: four-year institutions in Chicago, Illinois. In fall 2014, there were five four-year institutions in Chicago that were eligible for HSI status. These five HSIs were extremely diverse, as described by Núñez, Crisp, and Elizondo (2016). Four were small institutions, ranging in enrollment from approximately 1,400 to 2,800 undergraduate students. One was a midsize institution, with an approximate enrollment of 9,000. Four were private institutions, and one was public. Four were urban and one was suburban. By Carnegie classification, three were Master's Colleges and Universities, one was a Baccalaureate/Associate's College, and one was a Doctoral/Research University. One was a bilingual English–Spanish institution, and one was Roman Catholic. Recognizing that there is a tremendous amount of institutional diversity among HSIs, including control, size, type, religious affiliation, and location, focusing on four-year institutions was an essential way to compare and contrast institutions with a similar mission to graduate students with baccalaureate degrees. As a result of this mission, four-year institutions differ from two-year institutions, offer varying experiences for students, and produce different outcomes.

In this chapter, I provide an overview of the three colleges and universities that were included in the Midwest HSI Study. I also use the *Typology of HSI Organizational Identities* to classify the three HSIs, based strictly on my review of IPEDS data. I consider the three institutions in the study to be part of a population of HSIs, evolving within similar historical, political, and educational contexts (institutional perspective) (Garcia & Hudson, 2019). Yet the unique set of institutional characteristics that each one offers is worth considering separately (cultural perspective). Such details as the history, academic offerings, student services provided, and racial composition of the faculty and staff help to show the variations across three four-year HSIs in the same city. I remind the reader that the overall framing of this book is grounded in the theory of racialization. As such, I assume these HSIs have been assigned value based on their race, which is based on the race of the students they enroll. The racial makeup is connected to other institutional characteristics, such as selectivity and prestige, which is why I highlight these characteristics as well.

Azul City University

Azul City University (ACU; a pseudonym) is a four-year, midsize, public institution classified as a Master's College/University. It was founded in the late nineteenth century as one of the Midwest's first white teaching colleges and remained white until the 1960s, when people of color began forging their way into postsecondary education. ACU has grown to be a comprehensive university, offering bachelor's and master's programs in a variety of academic areas. Its stated mission is to offer high-quality academic programs to a broad spectrum of students while fostering their growth and development. The university emphasizes excellence in teaching and encourages faculty to practice applied research in academic and public spaces. As a result of its location in a large metropolitan area, the university serves a population that is racially diverse. Seen as a major asset, this diversity is utilized in a variety of ways to enrich the teaching and learning experience of students and to prepare them for a multiracial society.

ACU is a broad-access, less-selective institution, with an acceptance rate of nearly 60%. It is also one of the most affordable four-year HSIs in Chicago, with published annual tuition of approximately $9,000 in-state and of $17,000 out-of-state. In fall 2014, the institution was a commuter campus, as it did not offer on-campus residence facilities (this changed when the institution opened an on-campus residence hall in fall 2016). Nearly half of all undergraduates receive Pell Grants, and 30% receive federal loans. Of the first-time, full-time students entering in fall 2013, approximately 60% received Pell Grants averaging $4,500, and just under 20% received federal loans averaging $2,300. Very few students received institutional aid (less than 20%).

Based on these institutional characteristics, it can be assumed that ACU would struggle to graduate students, with institutional selectivity (Alon & Tienda, 2005) and student income (Rodríguez & Kelly, 2014) being two of the strongest predictors of graduation. Institutional resources are also a strong predictor of graduation rates for Latinx students (Garcia, 2013b); ACU's core revenue source is from tuition and fees (approximately $6,800 per FTE). As a state institution committed to access for the racially diverse regional population, ACU is not likely to increase tuition and fees, which may be inherently tied to its (in)ability to graduate these students. With six-year graduation rates under 20% for Latinx students, well below the national rate of 59%, ACU could be considered Hispanic-enrolling. Of course, this is complicated. Other aspects of ACU suggest that it might be serving Latinx students in ways other than those traditionally measured.

Academic Programs at ACU

ACU is a comprehensive university with more than eighty undergraduate and graduate programs. The campus has three main colleges: Arts and Sciences, Business and Management, and Education. Within these colleges, programs range from anthropology, history, and economics, to Earth sciences, chemistry, and mathematics. Some of the notable programs designed to center the experiences of specific populations include women's and gender studies (minor, BA); teaching bilingual/bicultural education (MAT); social justice (minor); lesbian, gay, bisexual, transgender, and queer studies (LGBTQ; minor); Latino and Latin American studies (minor, BA); Latin American literature and culture (MA); justice studies (BA); inner city studies (minor, BA, MA); community and teacher leaders (MA); Asian studies (minor); and African and African American studies (minor). In comparison to the other four institutions in the sample, ACU has the most extensive curricular offerings that center nondominant ways of knowing, which may be an important indicator of its ability to serve Latinx students (Garcia & Okhidoi, 2015).

In addition to its main campus, ACU has four satellite campuses, each with a unique focus. One is located in a predominantly Black neighborhood in the city, offering a minor, bachelor of arts, and master of arts in inner city studies education. A second site focuses on the Latinx community, offering educational opportunities in a culturally welcoming environment. It offers courses in fulfillment of bachelor's and master's programs offered through the main campus, along with academic and co-curricular support programs for Latinx students. It also has bilingual English–Spanish programs and courses in the evening, and it targets part-time, adult, and post-traditional students.[1] Outside of the city, ACU has a transfer center and a fourth satellite, with an emphasis on engaging the community in the mission of the university. The satellite campuses were strategically placed in Black and Latinx neighborhoods with a mission to serve these populations.

Student Support Programs at ACU

ACU stresses a commitment to student success and belonging, which is reflected in its university-sponsored programs and services, including a learning support center, advising center, and transitional support center. It also offers programs that specifically cater to minoritized populations, including federally sponsored TRiO programs, internally developed support programs specifically for racially and economically minoritized students, and a program that trains Latinx graduate students to be administrative leaders in higher education. ACU also has an intercultural affairs center that houses six centers: Undocumented Student Resource Center, Latinx Resource Center, African/African American Resource Center, Asian and Global Resource Center, LGBTQA Resource Center, and Women's Resource Center. As a collective, the intercultural affairs center strives to foster success for historically marginalized groups on campus through educational programming, skill development workshops, mentoring, and other culturally relevant programming. Of the four-year HSIs in the sample, ACU is the only one with a specific cultural center for Latinx students. There are also more than seventy student organizations at ACU, with several that support the development and success of minoritized groups on campus, including the National Society of Hispanic MBAs, SACNAS (an organization that advances Chicanos/Hispanics and Native Americans in Science), the Puerto Rican Union, and an undocumented student organization. Again, these culturally relevant resources may be an indicator of ACU's ability to serve Latinx students (Garcia & Okhidoi, 2015).

Compositional Diversity at ACU

In fall 2013, the undergraduate head count was nearly 9,000. The compositional diversity of the institution is notable, with 37% identifying as white, 35% as Latinx, 10% as Black or African American, and 9.5% as Asian. By enrollment status, nearly 60% percent of students are enrolled full-time and approximately 40% are enrolled part-time. The racial makeup of the part-time students is very close to the overall enrollment, with Black or African American students and white students being slightly overrepresented in the part-time student population. A large percentage of students at ACU are also low income, with approximately half receiving Pell Grants. Fifty-five percent of undergraduates are traditional college age (24 and under), and about 55% are female. Most students are from the state of Illinois.

The composition of the faculty is less diverse than the student population. Of the instructional staff with faculty status, 35% are nontenure stream, 25% are on the tenure track, and 40% have earned tenure. Among the faculty, 63% identify as white, 11% as Latinx, 7% as Black or African American, and 11% as Asian. While these racial disparities are considerable, they are slightly lower for faculty on the tenure track, with this group identifying as 48% white, 16% Latinx, 7% Black or African American, and 15% Asian. This is an important shift, as it suggests that the institution is actively hiring more faculty of color in tenure-track positions. This will eventually lead to a shift in the racial disparities of the tenured faculty, among whom 62% identified as white, 11% as Latinx, 8% as Black or African American, and 14% as Asian.

The administration is slightly more diverse than the faculty. At the management level, 55% of administrators identify as white, 18% as Latinx, 14% as Black or African American, and 8% as Asian. It is notable that there is a larger percentage of Black or African American managers than students. Within the academic and student affairs staff, the racial makeup is even more diverse, with 38% identifying as white, 25% as Latinx, 24% as Black or African American, and 5% as Asian. This has implications, as students may be more likely to interact with staff at this level, meaning they are more likely to see people with similar racial backgrounds working in offices that provide services.

ACU as an HSI

U.S. News and World Report has recognized ACU as one of the most ethnically diverse institutions in the Midwest. It is one of the oldest HSIs in the Midwest, with federal recognition since the mid-1990s. ACU has also been a member of the Hispanic Association of Colleges and Universities since the early 1990s. The institution has received multiple HSI grants from various federal agencies as well as state funding in order to implement HSI initiatives. It received developing HSI grants from the Department of Agriculture and the Department of Education, as well as a Department of Education Developing HSIs cooperative grant with a local community college, a Title V Post-baccalaureate grant, and a Department of Education College Cost Reduction and Access Act (CCRAA) for HSIs grant. With each of these grants, the institution has been able to develop programs and services that enhance its ability to serve the university community as well as the surrounding community. ACU has a government relations administrator who actively works to promote the HSI designation and seeks out funding opportunities that support capacity-building efforts to better serve Latinx students. ACU publicly identifies as an HSI and considers its HSI designation to be an important "quick fact" on its website. Taking all institutional characteristics into consideration, I categorize ACU as *Latinx-enhancing*, meaning it does not do well in producing outcomes that are legitimized by white standards (e.g., retention and graduation rates), but it offers an experience that enhances the racial and cultural ways of knowing of Latinx students (Garcia, 2018b).

Amarillo Private College

Amarillo Private College (APC; a pseudonym) is a small private institution classified as a Baccalaureate/Associate's College offering a few bachelor's and associate's degrees. APC was founded in the 1980s as a dual-language/bilingual institution with the specific mission to provide academic and vocational training to the growing number of Latinx people in the city. In this sense, APC is the only institution in the sample that was not founded as white and did not *become* racially minoritized; rather, its historical mission has been to serve Latinx people. The institution avails itself to a racially diverse student population, but it focuses on the Latinx community, with the goal of strengthening ethnic identity and reinforcing cultural knowledge. The founders are pioneers in bilingual higher education, creating the institution after spending nearly ten years researching, observing, and working with the Latinx community. APC's model is a transitional bilingual program, often seen at the primary school level, with students first enrolling in classes that help them learn English before transitioning into dual-language English–Spanish classes. In addition to the main campus, APC has four satellite campuses, three in the city and one in a suburb with a large Latinx population. At its five sites, APC is able to offer hands-on education and support services to students.

APC is an open access institution, only requiring the equivalence of a high school degree and a minimum age of seventeen in order to enroll. The published tuition is approximately $9,800 per year, making it one of the most affordable private institutions in Chicago. A majority of students receive some form of financial aid, and 70% of all undergraduates receive federal Pell Grants. In fall 2013, 89% of all first-time, full-time students received financial aid, with 82% receiving Pell Grants, 27% receiving grants through the Illinois Monetary Award Program (MAP), and 74% receiving institutional aid. No students received federal or other loans in fall 2013, which is something the institution is proud of and striving to maintain. It is a commuter campus, with no on-campus housing facilities. A majority of APC's revenues are from tuition and fees (approximately $8,900 per FTE) and a majority of the institution's core expenses are for instruction (approximately $5,200 per FTE) and institutional support (approximately $4,200 per FTE), both of which may influence graduation rates at the institution.

Based on the characteristics of students likely to attend APC, it would be expected that graduation rates might not be as high as the national average, as income is a strong predictor of graduation (Rodríguez & Kelly, 2014). Yet, at the institutional level, being private is a positive predictor of graduation (Scott, Bailey, & Kienzi, 2006). Other institutional characteristics, however, tend to be negative predictors, including lower selectivity (Alon & Tienda, 2005) and fewer institutional resources (Ryan, 2004; Webber & Ehrenberg, 2010). Although APC's six-year graduation rates are quite low, at 24%, this number may not be an accurate indicator of effectiveness for the institution. Because many of its students are post-traditional and may not be first-time, full-time students, the six-year graduation rate may not capture them. This is a flaw inherent within a racialized system, one in which white normative standards (e.g., six-year graduation rates) are used to assess the value of all institutions, regardless of their unique mission to provide access to post-secondary education for the Latinx community.

Academic Programs at APC

APC offers a limited number of academic programs, including three bachelor's degrees and ten associate's degrees. The bachelor's programs are a bachelor of arts in hospitality management, a bachelor of arts in psychology, and a bachelor of social work. The bachelor of social work program emphasizes social justice and fieldwork experience in the community, while the bachelor of arts in hospitality management focuses on building students' skills around business and culinary arts, with the goal of graduating students who can immediately work within the field upon completion. The bachelor of arts in psychology prepares students to work directly with people in a variety of settings. Two associate of arts programs prepare students to transfer to four-year colleges and universities, with such areas of concentration as business administration, social service, child development, addiction counseling, Spanish, and criminal justice. The institution also offers seven associates of applied sciences degrees to be used for skill development and immediate entry into the field; areas of concentration include accounting, administrative assistant, computer information systems, culinary arts, early childhood education, and respiratory therapy. The tenth associate's program is in general studies. The curriculum is focused on graduating students who can immediately get jobs in their applied fields, which is a notable outcome for students. The degree offerings are vocational in nature, similar to those traditionally seen at Historically Black Colleges and Universities in the past, which have been criticized for limiting opportunities for the Black community (Anderson, 1988). APC's program offerings, therefore, may reinforce the systemic racial hierarchy.

In addition to the bachelor's and associate's degree programs, APC offers pre-college programs, including a General Education Development (GED) option. The ten-week GED program is offered in English and Spanish and is intended to prepare students to enter one of the degree programs at the institution. APC also has a workforce development program that aims to be the largest provider of workforce training to employees in the metropolitan area. Again, while these programs can be considered essential to advancing the educational training of the Latinx community, they further subjugate the institution by race, because these types of programs are not typically valued in the same way as bachelor's, master's, and doctoral degrees are within the field of higher education. In other words, colleges and universities are recognized as elite based on their production of four-year bachelor's degrees and graduate degrees.

Student Support Programs at APC

APC offers basic student support services, including an admissions office, financial aid office, the bursar's office, and advising. Once students are admitted, they are assigned an academic advisor who assists them through a variety of services, such as academic planning, student complaints, and learning (dis)ability assistance. APC also offers tutoring services; a testing center, which coordinates and administers placement tests and academic related tests; and a career and transfer center. Finally, APC offers affordable childcare for children ages three to twelve. While it does not have specialized cultural programs, such as a Latinx resource center, the campus offers students an individualized experience, including interaction with bilingual/bicultural staff members who get to know students on a personal level. APC is able to offer this type of experience because the campus is small, with the goal of making students feel welcomed.

Compositional Diversity at APC

Undergraduate enrollment in fall 2013 was approximately 1,600. The institution is unique in that it primarily enrolls Latinx students, with 87% identifying as Latinx. In comparison, less than 1% identify as white, 2.5% as Black or African American, and 1% as Asian. By enrollment status, 71% identify as full-time students and 29% as part-time. Seventy percent of all undergraduates are low-income students, as indicated by the number who receive Pell Grants. A majority of students are female (77%) and post-traditional; the average age is thirty-one.

While the composition of the faculty is more diverse than the other four-year HSIs in Chicago, it does not match the composition of the student population. The institution does not offer tenure-track positions. Among the instructional staff with faculty status, 48% identify as Latinx, 38% identify as white, 3.5% as Black or African American, and 3.5% as Asian. The composition of the administration is more closely aligned with the diversity of the students. At the management level, 77% identify as Latinx, 18% as white, and 4.5% as Black or African American. There are no self-identified Asian managers on campus. There is very little "racial diversity" within the academic and student affairs staff, as 97% identify as Latinx and 3% identify as white. Notably, the president of APC is a Spanish-speaking Latino male who is actively engaged with the Latinx community in the regional area and has served as the president of the Illinois LAtino Council on Higher Education (ILACHE). Other high-level administrators are also Spanish-speaking Latinxs, some of whom are considered to be the founders of the institution and who remain steadfast in their commitment to serve the Latinx community in the region. A large percentage of the faculty and staff are also Spanish-speaking.

APC as an HSI

Although APC was not founded as a federally designated HSI, it was founded to serve Latinxs in the regional area through bilingual education, accessible locations, and convenient course offerings. It is one of the few HSIs still in existence that was specifically founded with the mission to serve the Latinx community. It was one of the original institutional members of HACU and has been recognized by HACU for its excellence as an HSI. APC has also been awarded at least one Department of Education Title V Developing HSIs grant. While APC has assumed the federal designation, its historical mission of being a bilingual institution and serving the Latinx community in Chicago exemplify it as Latinx-serving, regardless of federal designation. In other words, APC will continue to enroll and educate Latinx students, with or without the designation, as these values are engrained in its mission. As such, it may actually be rejecting the dominant white racial narrative of postsecondary institutions. In reviewing its institutional characteristics, I contend that APC is *Latinx-serving* (Garcia, 2018b). This is complicated, as the outcomes that are legitimized by white standards, such as six-year graduation rates, are lower than the national average at APC. Yet the six-year graduation rate may be inaccurate for APC because the measure does do not capture students who are not first-time, full-time students to the institution. APC enrolls post-traditional students, who are not likely to fit the first-time, full-time enrollment category, making the six-year graduation rate unreliable. Moreover, as one of the few institutions actually founded to serve the Latinx community, through language and engagement, having a Latinx-serving identity is a natural function of the institution.

Rosado Private University

Rosado Private University (RPU; a pseudonym) is a small private institution classified as a Master's College/University. It's an urban, comprehensive university that provides a professional, career-focused undergraduate education. It offers associate's, bachelor's, and master's degrees. RPU was founded and chartered outside of Chicago in the 1960s, but eventually moved into the Chicago area and merged with another small school that was founded in the early twentieth century. Since its founding, RPU has continued to grow, adding nine additional campuses across Illinois. RPU's stated mission is to prepare students to become practitioners who are socially responsible in their communities and who serve as foundations in their families. RPU values experiential learning and has an institute that works with students and the community to develop community-based projects.

RPU is a selective institution, with a 24% acceptance rate. The published tuition is approximately $25,000 per year. For students who live on campus in university-owned facilities (10%), the annual cost is approximately $40,000. A majority of the students (94%) receive grants and scholarships, and 60% of all undergraduates receive Pell Grants. A large percentage (82%) also receive federal student loans. In addition to state and federal financial support, RPU awards approximately $28 million in institutional aid annually. In fall 2013, 82% of first-time, full-time students received institutional aid, with the average amount being $8,400. In that same cohort, 88% received student loans, with the average amount being $7,200, and 70% received Pell Grants, with the average amount being $4,200.

This snapshot suggests that students at RPU rely on a diversified financial aid package that will likely contribute to their persistence and graduation, since grants and scholarship, as well as the amount of these awards, have a positive effect on graduation for Latinx students (Alon, 2007). A majority (80%) of the institution's revenues come from tuition and fees (approximately $16,000 per FTE), which could negatively affect its graduation rates (Ryan, 2004; Webber & Ehrenberg, 2010). RPU's high six-year graduation rates (55% for Latinx students) are likely indicative of its status as a private, selective institution. As such, from a higher education population perspective, the institution is likely to be valued and rewarded for being a good server of Latinx students, regardless of other elements present in the institution.

Academic Programs

RPU has eight academic colleges and offers seventeen fields of study. In 2011, RPU introduced a liberal arts curriculum designed for students who wish to obtain a degree in the major fields of arts, humanities, social sciences, fine arts, mathematics, and natural sciences. The Graduate School of Business offers three graduate programs, and the remaining seven academic colleges offer a total of five bachelor's programs in the areas of business, culinary arts, nursing, health care, and technology. As a practitioner-focused institution, degrees are designed to develop high-performing practitioners. The field of business is the most dominant at RPU, with the most degree offerings in this area. RPU stresses the use of an experiential learning model. Moreover, RPU operates on an accelerated timetable so that students can graduate in four years or less. RPU does not offer courses that focus on the racialized experiences of students, meaning that white voices continue to be dominant within the curriculum.

Student Support Programs at RPU

RPU offers basic student support services, including an admissions office, financial aid office, tutoring services, student support services, and career services. In particular, RPU emphasizes financial aid assistance and career placement. It offers an extensive staff of financial aid experts who assist students from pre-matriculation, through enrollment, and into graduation. RPU also offers comprehensive career services programs, including a four-course curriculum that students are required to complete. The four courses focus on resume and skill development to prepare students to enter the workforce upon graduation. RPU also has student housing available for 1,680 students and study abroad opportunities specific to different majors. While a majority of these services are offered at each of its ten campuses, the delivery of services looks different on each campus, since each site has its own distinct needs and vary in number of students served.

Other areas of student support include Student Support Services, which is funded by a federal grant sponsored by the Department of Education. Specifically, Student Support Services targets low-income, first-generation students, offering one-on-one academic and personal advising, academic skills assessment, study skills workshops, career development, standardized test preparation (for graduate school admission), and a computer lab. RPU also has a TRiO program that includes the Educational Talent Search, Student Support Services, and Upward Bound. Through these programs, RPU does outreach to low-income and first-generation high school students in the city. Finally, RPU supports more than forty student organizations, with at least three focused on the Latinx community, and a few others that have an emphasis on racialized students.

Compositional Diversity at RPU

In fall 2013, the undergraduate head count was approximately 2,800, with notable compositional diversity. Of the undergraduate population, 38% identified as white, 27% identified as Latinx, 28% identified as Black or African American, and 3% as Asian. Compared to the other four-year HSIs in Chicago, RPU has the most significant Black population, although the Asian population is much lower. Approximately 50% of the population identifies as female. Sixty percent are low income, as indicated by Pell Grant eligibility. By enrollment, 95% are full-time students, with a majority (75%) of the students considered "traditional" college age (24 or under).

While the racial composition of students is quite diverse, the faculty, staff, and administration at RPU are lagging behind in this regard. Of the instructional staff with faculty status, 76% identify as white, while only 2% identify as Latinx, 9% as Black or African American, and 13% as Asian. These numbers are quite staggering when compared to the racial identities of the students. RPU does not have a tenure system. The administration is also predominantly white (77%). About 7.5% identify as Latinx, 11% as Black or African American, and 4% as Asian. Notably, the student and academic affairs staff is more diverse, with about half (49%) identifying as white, 26% as Latinx, 18% as Black or African American, and 2.5% as Asian.

RPU as an HSI

RPU has been recognized as one of the most diverse institutions in the Midwest and is federally recognized as an HSI. RPU has been designated as an HSI since the late 1990s and received at least one Title V grant in 1999 in order to develop its management information system, strengthen its academic programs, and establish an endowment program. The institution has also partnered with Amarillo Private College in order to establish a 2 + 2 program through which students can complete two years of coursework at APC before transferring to RPU. I categorize RPU as *Latinx-producing*, meaning it is equitably producing outcomes that are legitimized by white standards, yet it operates in a racially and culturally neutral way (Garcia, 2018b). With the institution seemingly serving Latinx (and other racially minoritized) students well as measured by graduation rates, the institution does not seem to be taking steps to identify with its racially minoritized organizational identity.

HSIs in Chicago: Reinforcing or Challenging the Dominant Narrative?

While scholars agree that institutional diversity is a staple of the US postsecondary system (Birnbaum, 1983; Harris, 2013), little attention has been paid to the racialization of colleges and universities, or to the unintended consequences of this process. The stratification of the postsecondary educational system has historically privileged white institutions while simultaneously subjugating racially minoritized institutions, such as HSIs. This is evident in the criticism HSIs receive for not equitably graduating Latinx students, with some scholars arguing that merely providing access to Latinx students is an inadequate measure of serving these students. This of course is based on institutionalized ways of knowing, with effectiveness being determined at the field level and in comparison to other institutions. In reviewing the institutional and student characteristics of the three institutions in the Midwest HSI study, it becomes evident that this type of comparative evaluation disadvantages HSIs when strictly using white normative standards. Evaluating institutional effectiveness based solely on graduation rates ignores other indicators that predict graduation, including students' income level (Rodríguez & Kelly, 2014) and institutional resources (Garcia, 2013b), both of which are intertwined with race in a way that disadvantages students of color.

As the number of HSIs increases, there is a need to evaluate these institutions as unique racialized entities. Even further, there is a need to center a racialized narrative that disrupts the white ideologies grounded in research based on white institutions. The four-year HSIs in Chicagoland created a suitable situation for doing this, particularly as they were at different stages of their evolution as racially minoritized entities. Grounded in a social constructionist perspective, I allowed members at each of the three institutions to make meaning of an HSI organizational identity, with an emphasis on better understanding the cultural indicators of this identity. In the next three chapters, I use primary data collected through interviews, focus groups, and direct observations, as well as secondary data from document reviews and existing literature on HSIs, in order to construct counterstories for each institution. In doing so, I question the extent to which HSIs in the Midwest are reinforcing the racial order of postsecondary institutions rather than challenging the dominant white narrative about postsecondary institutions.

THREE

Enhancing the Cultural Experience of Latinx Students

COMMON MEASURES of postsecondary institutional effectiveness include persistence (progress) and graduation (outcomes) (Dougherty & Reddy, 2013; Jones et al., 2017). It is generally accepted that if postsecondary institutions have high persistence and graduation rates, they are effective institutions; if they don't, they aren't. We rarely question these as white normative measures, determined within a backdrop of whiteness, under exclusionary conditions, and without consideration for the input variables of students of color. Researchers, legislators, and institutional leaders have grappled with what it means for Hispanic-Serving Institutions to effectively serve Latinx students by turning to these commonly used measures of institutional effectiveness—persistence and graduation—with little discussion about how these measures may be a reflection of sociohistoric racist practices. Scholars have noted the racial inequities in persistence and graduation rates of students attending HSIs in comparison to non-HSIs, and they have been quick to suggest that this is an indicator that HSIs are ineffective in serving Latinx (and other racialized) students, rather than questioning the validity of these measures. Yet persistence and graduation are complex measures that are reflective of institutional type.

Among first-time, full-time degree-seeking students in 2014–2015, the overall first-year retention rate for those attending a two-year institution was 61% and for those attending a four-year institution was 81% (National Center for Education Statistics [NCES], 2017). These numbers suggest that in the aggregate, first-year persistence is an issue for all institutions, as anywhere between 20% and 40% of students stop attending their first institution after just one academic year. Disaggregating persistence rates at the four-year level reveals huge disparities between open access institutions (59%) and the most selective institutions (96%), suggesting that first-year persistence is a major issue for less-selective, broad-access institutions, such as HSIs.

Six-year graduation rates show additional concerns, as the average percentage of first-time, full-time bachelor's degree–seeking students at four-year institutions who completed a degree program in 2014–2015 was 59% (NCES, 2017). There are also huge inequities based on institutional selectivity, with broad-access institutions (those that are either open access or accept at least 50% of applicants) graduating students at rates between 32% and 62%, while more selective institutions have six-year graduation rates of 70% to 88%. What the numbers reveal is that persistence and graduation are major concerns for nearly all institutions, although less-selective, broad-access institutions struggle more than selective institutions do.

The HSI Dilemma: Institutional Characteristics Lead to Student Outcomes

HSIs, which are most likely to be less-selective, broad-access institutions, will inevitably struggle to graduate students, not because they lack an historic mission to serve Latinx students, but because they are less-selective, broad-access institutions. In seeking to reframe what it means for an institution to serve Latinx students, this reality cannot be overlooked. Evidence shows that institutional selectivity is a strong predictor of graduation, even for racially and economically disadvantaged students (Alon & Tienda, 2005; Andrew, 2017; Gansemer-Topf & Schuh, 2006). Yet there are huge racial disparities in the enrollment of students, with highly selective institutions enrolling mostly white students (Carnevale & Strohl, 2013).

Knowing that HSIs are likely to have lower persistence and six-year graduation rates than racially white institutions do because of institutional characteristics such as selectivity and accessibility complicates any effort to determine the effectiveness of these institutions with regard to serving Latinx students, particularly if academic progress and outcome measures are the main considerations in determining effectiveness. As a result of sociohistorical factors, such as educational segregation and restrictive language policies, persistence and retention processes for Latinx students (and all students of color) are more complex than they are for white students (Garcia, 2018a). These factors must be considered alongside the issues of persistence and graduation for Latinx students as measures of institutional effectiveness. Despite what early retention models suggested, scholars contend that students of color should not be expected to academically and socially integrate into the mainstream, white culture of postsecondary institutions, while simultaneously leaving their racial, ethnic, and cultural ways of knowing behind (Hurtado & Carter, 1997; Muñoz & Maldonado, 2011; Rendon, Jalomo, & Nora, 2000). In reality, becoming fully integrated into an institution could be detrimental for racially minoritized students, as students of color often rely on out-of-college networks, such as families and peers, to thrive within college (e.g., Ceballo, 2004; Easley, Bianco, & Leech, 2012). Scholars have argued that institutions should be concerned with Latinx students' sense of belonging on campus, rather than their full integration (e.g., Hurtado & Carter, 1997; Hurtado & Ponjuan, 2005; Strayhorn, 2008).

HSIs as Culturally Enhancing Spaces

Empirical evidence suggests that HSIs are progressing, albeit slowly, in recognizing that enhancing the racial and cultural experience of Latinx students is part of their role as institutions that enroll large percentages of minoritized students. I call this a "Latinx-enhancing" identity, or one in which the institution recognizes and provides a racially and culturally engaging environment for students (Garcia, 2017). In arguing for a more nuanced approach to understanding how HSIs embrace their organizational identity, I suggest that providing an experience that is racially and culturally enhancing for minoritized students is a form of serving them (Garcia, 2016, 2017). This aligns with decades of research on the ways in which white institutions should provide spaces that not only recognize minoritized students' ways of knowing and being, but enhance their sense of belonging, engagement, racial and ethnic identity, and personal knowledge of self (e.g., Hurtado et al., 2012; Museus, 2014; Rendon et al., 2000).

Although a mere 2% of HSIs offer racial and ethnocentric curricular options (Cole, 2011), numerous articles have shown that, on a case-by-case basis, faculty at HSIs are starting to think about the unique curricular needs of Latinx students. Kiasatpour and Lasley (2008), for example, compared political science faculty teaching at HSIs in Texas to those teaching at national and "other" institutions in Texas and found that those teaching at HSIs were more likely to focus on Latinx-specific politics and Mexico–US relations than faculty from the other two institutional types were, suggesting that the faculty at HSIs understand that students are more likely to be engaged and learn when the content is of interest to them and recognizes their racial and cultural experiences. Faculty teaching at HSIs were also more likely to incorporate service learning and civic engagement activities into their classroom, and to utilize group activities and free-writing exercises (Kiasatpour & Lasley, 2008).

Pedagogically, faculty are also showing signs of intentionality in their teaching approach. Lara and Lara (2012) note that within their criminal justice and chemistry classrooms at an HSI, they "pepper [their] lessons with Spanish, Chican@ history, *colonia* knowledge—elements to which many of [their] students can *relate*" (p. 179). They stress the importance of Latinx students staying connected to the communities that nurtured them and encourage students to make a difference in those communities (Lara & Lara, 2012). Similarly, faculty at the University of Texas at San Antonio have intentionally implemented what they call "pedagogy for equity," which includes encouraging students to understand their identities in relation to their home communities, serving as role models to students with similar identities as themselves, and responding to students' racial, ethnic, and cultural forms of expression (Núñez et al., 2010).

In addition to curricular and pedagogical changes, there is evidence of programs that are more intentionally considering the unique ways of knowing of Latinx students. Again, these examples are on a case-by-case basis, yet they are emerging within HSIs and have been documented, both in research and in practice.[1] Examples of programs that use a Latinx lens include Adams State University's Higher Education Administration and Leadership (HEAL) program, which was created after the institution became an HSI as a way to educate and train future leaders for all Minority-Serving Institutions (Freeman, 2015). Nevada State College's Nepantla program is an outreach and recruitment program that not only recognizes Latinx students' racial and cultural ways of knowing, but also encourages them to resist the dominant narrative about who goes to college and to embrace the space "in between" high school and college, which is full of unfamiliar challenges (Natividad, 2015). Garcia and Okhidoi (2015) discuss how one HSI in the Southwest centered its advising practices on the experiences of minoritized students by decentralizing their Educational Opportunity Program (EOP) and providing access to EOP services to all students in all majors, regardless of income or college generational status.

These are just a few of the numerous ways in which faculty, staff, and students attending HSIs are beginning to make sense of what it means to serve Latinx students beyond the federal designation and beyond graduation rates. While retention and graduation rates will always be important indicators of institutional effectiveness, I suggest that an organizational identity for serving students is more complex than traditional progress and outcome indicators (Garcia, 2016, 2017, 2018b). Enacting an organizational identity for effectively serving Latinx students may ultimately be connected to graduation rates and post-baccalaureate enrollment and job placement (Garcia, 2017), even as it also connects to culturally engaging practices (Garcia, 2016; Garcia & Okhidoi, 2015).

Azul City University as Culturally Enhancing

In this chapter, I provide a counterstory for Azul City University, which has been a federally recognized HSI for over twenty years. In serving the Chicagoland, it enrolls a diverse mix of minoritized groups, including Latinx, low-income, and undocumented students. Data from IPEDS, however, reveal that it is struggling to graduate all students (Garcia, 2018b). Using data from historical documents at the institution, reports produced by external organizations, one-on-one interviews with faculty and staff at the institution, focus groups and one-on-one interviews with students, and ethnographic observations, this chapter's counterstory is a composite story, based on a combination of the data collected, the extant literature on the topic, and my own personal and professional experiences (Solórzano & Yosso, 2002).

The counterstory lays out what it looks like for an institution to en-act a Latinx-enhancing organizational identity, or one that enhances the cultural and racial ways of knowing of Latinx college students through its practices, but does not produce racially equitable outcomes for students (Garcia, 2017). This counterstory is intended to be liberating for the people within the institution, who spent a great deal of time talking about the ways in which ACU is not an effective HSI without recognizing that their measures of effectiveness are based on an institutionalized perspective and grounded in whiteness. This counterstory is narrated by Carmen, a graduate student enrolled in a master's in education program that trains graduate students to be administrators at postsecondary institutions, with a focus on HSIs and other MSIs.[2] It opens up at a town hall meeting hosted by Carmen and Andrea to talk about the campus's designation as an HSI.

The Town Hall Meeting

As I work with the person from technology to do one last sound check and to make sure that our Prezi presentation is working, my nerves begin to take hold of me. I am excited about this town hall meeting, which was the result of a class project from last semester in which a professor in our master's program had us learn about HSIs in the United States and develop a list of policy recommendations for administrators. When I started the master's program, I didn't know what an HSI was. I got my bachelor's degree from a small liberal arts college in California that actually was an HSI, but nobody ever talked about that. I mean, it was cool, all my friends spoke Spanish, except for a few *pochas*, but even they tried, fitting right in. We had a mariachi band at graduation, which my family loved.[3] So, yea, I felt like I belonged there, but I didn't really think about it being "Hispanic-serving."

Completing this project gave me the opportunity to learn about the history of HSIs and the Hispanic Association of Colleges and Universities (HACU), which was formed in 1986 to advocate for Latinx students and HSIs. I also learned that my home state of California has 159 HSIs and 56 emerging HSIs. Wow! I was shocked! But not really, as it kind of makes sense that a state with so many Latinxs would have a lot of HSIs. It's like common sense; of course places like California, Texas, Florida, and New York would have a lot of HSIs. But what I also learned through this project was that states like Illinois and Kansas and Massachusetts have a growing number of HSIs. So that's dope. It's like the browning of colleges and universities.

People enter the auditorium where the town hall is being held. I get a little nervous, because the room seems to be mostly faculty and staff. We wanted students to attend, as their voices matter; they start to trickle in, generally sitting in the way back of the room and immediately pulling out their phones. Our professor motions us to get the program started, because people are getting anxious. As a commuter campus serving post-traditional students, we have to be respectful of people's time; they have busy lives and don't want to spend their whole afternoon on campus. We thank everyone for attending and give shout outs to all the faculty and staff who supported the town hall, including the vice president of student affairs, the director of the multicultural center, the director of the Latino Cultural Center, the director of the Undocumented Student Center, and the director of government relations, who we found, through this assignment, knows a lot about HSIs; she's like the *reyna* (queen) of HSIs.

I start the presentation, giving an overview of HSIs, including their history and development. I quickly move into our status as an HSI. I declare, "The purpose of this town hall meeting is to first talk about what we are already doing as an HSI, but then to talk about what we *should* be doing. How many of you knew that ACU was an HSI before you came here today?" Most of the participants raise their hands. "OK, great, then I expect y'all to have ideas about what we should be doing as an HSI. In conducting research for our class, we determined that ACU has three strengths and three challenges that should be recognized and addressed."

Structural Support for Enhancing the Cultural Experience of Students

I fumble with the Prezi, getting lost and a little bit dizzy as I try to find the strengths slides. I apologize, "Sorry y'all." I find my place, but I'm nervous. "Strength number one: We have signature Latinx support programs; programs that have served Latinx students for over forty years. We have a program that admits students who do not meet the admissions criteria of the university. That program began as a grassroots effort, with Puerto Rican students fighting for their right to gain admission to this university, back when it was all white. That program provides transitional support to students, both academic and emotional, including a class that students take that introduces them to the university.

"We also have a satellite campus, located two miles from the main campus in a predominantly Latinx community. The main goal of that campus is to bring the university to the Latinx community. When it was opened over forty years ago, it offered GED programs, but now students can earn their degree by taking classes there, in a small environment and with staff and faculty who speak Spanish and understand their racial and cultural needs. They also offer classes in the evening and on the weekends, to make it more convenient and accessible to the community. These programs are historic on this campus; they have been around longer than all of us. More recently we have established a Latino Cultural Center and a center for undocumented students. We are one of the only campus in the United States that has a center and a full-time staff member dedicated to working with and for undocumented students. We learned that administrators and students and local politicians fought for these centers. Our collective resistance efforts cannot be overlooked, as the white people have never given us anything that we didn't fight for. How many of you were aware of these programs and the history of activism on this campus?" Nearly three-fourths of the participants raise their hands. I smile and continue.

"As we did research for this project, we talked to people on campus about what it means to be an HSI and we found that these signature Latinx programs were mentioned a lot. Two people stressed that we were an HSI even before the federal designation. They said that these signature programs for Latinxs have nothing to do with our designation as an HSI. The university didn't say, 'Oh we're an HSI, so let's create these signature Latinx programs.' The HSI designation came after the fact. A good way to think about it is that we were already an HSI, before the government told us we were. We don't need anybody to tell us we're Latinx!!" The crowd erupts in laughter. "But in doing our research, we learned that we have been taking Uncle Sam's money too. Thank you, Uncle Sam." The laughter continues.

"This brings me to strength number two: We have signature Latinx academic programs. At the undergraduate level, we have the Latino Studies program. That program is interdisciplinary, with faculty from other departments teaching in the program. It started as a certificate program, but faculty fought for it to become a minor, and then a major. The program is continuing to gain traction on campus. We also learned that women and gender studies, justice studies, and social work are signature social justice programs on campus. The faculty teach about social justice issues and Latinx issues, and many of them are aware of the institution's designation as an HSI. We talked to some white faculty in those departments who are more woke than some of the faculty of color around here." More laughter from the crowd. "Seriously, the white faculty in those departments don't play. They talk about oppression and racism and immigration and the criminal justice system and Black Lives Matter. Fists up for the white people doing racial justice work around here." Participants raise their fists in the air.

"We also have a master's program in education that is training future administrators to work at HSIs and other MSIs, called ENLACE. It provides scholarships to Latinx students to enroll in a two-year program with a concentration in higher education. Students who get the scholarship take three classes that focus on the issues of educating Latinx college students in the twenty-first century. My peers and I are in the program, and we learned about HSIs through one of our classes. This town hall meeting is part of our final class project. Thank you for being here, or we might fail the class." Again laughter erupts. I smile and say, "*Es un chiste* (It's a joke), we already passed the class. We also learned a lot about HSIs from staff on campus who graduated from this master's program. We consider this a strength because it is a 'grow your own' type of program; you know, grow your own administrators who are all woke and conscious of Latinx people and their struggles. Sounds like a good idea, right?" People clap. "We believe these two strengths, having signature Latinx academic programs and Latinx support programs, makes us Hispanic-serving."

I move into the third and final strength. "Strength number three: We have taken steps to recognize our HSI designation. We have a director of government relations who is connected to federal agencies that are funding grants for HSIs and who keeps us posted on those opportunities. As a result, we have applied for and received a lot of HSI grants, including grants from the Department of Education, USDA [Department of Agriculture], HUD [Housing and Urban Development], and local foundations, as well as from the state. These grants have created numerous opportunities for everyone on campus. One grant was used to start a writing-intensive program. With the grant, the English department established a Writing Center and continues to fund that program, even without the grant money. One grant was used to establish the Science Support Center. Have y'all been to the science center? They have tutors for math and science classes; they have a computer lab; they help students find research opportunities; and they help students get into graduate school. That center was started with a grant, but now the university supports it. We learned about a lot of HSI grants that have established support programs, not just for Latinx students, but for all students, because all students on this campus need support." The crowd snaps in agreement.

"Also, the administration has been supportive of our efforts to become an HSI." I hear some moaning and tussling in the crowd as I make this statement. "Before y'all start throwing *chingasos* (punches), hear me out. We know that the administration needs to do better, and if you're an administrator in this room, do better! Administrators, and particularly non-Latinx administrators, have not always been supportive of our efforts to become an HSI. *Pero, la reyna* [of HSIs], who works directly with the president and other administrators, feels strongly about the support she has received from at least two of our last few presidents. They have been vocal about their support, both at the federal level and with HACU, and they have been influential in these spaces. Yes, administrators have made some bad decisions that go against the HSI designation, like establishing a residence hall despite the fact that we know Black and Brown students at this school can't afford to live there, but they have also been supportive in other ways. The current president knows that we are an HSI and supports the collective work to be Latinx-serving. Admittedly, this support comes in waves, with those committed to being an HSI feeling more supported some years and less supported other years."

I notice that some of the faculty are not happy about my comments. Admittedly, the faculty we talked to were critical of the administration and questioned the administration's support of us being an HSI and supporting Latinx students. But I continue, standing by my statements. "One indicator of this support is reflected in the fact that the president recently approved a special position for HSI initiatives. This person will be a full-time, tenured faculty member on campus who will report directly to the provost. This person will help to coordinate HSI efforts;

work with media and communications to figure out an effective way to make people aware of ACU's status as an HSI; work with government relations to promote federal, local, and foundation grants on campus; and serve as an advisor to the provost on HSI issues. Also, this person will help us sort out our own confusion about what it means to be an HSI. This is a huge win. From our research, we found that very few institutions have this type of position on campus. We're trailblazers." Snaps from the crowd.

Inhibitors to Enhancing the Cultural Experience of Students

I continue to move through my presentation. "Despite these strengths, we also face a number of challenges. Challenge number one: Black and Brown folks on this campus don't get along! This was surprising and sad for us to learn about as we talked to people. But these tensions are legitimate and should be acknowledged. Historically, this campus has had resources for the Black community, including satellite campuses, cultural centers, and outreach and transition programs. We have also had Black administrators and a Black president, which is such an important part of our history as an institution. But the dramatic shift in the population of Latinxs in Chicago is now reflected in the population of the university. Even further, the institution seems to reflect the segregation of the city—the segregation that divides Black and Brown communities. We are a microcosm of the city.

"We know that Black and Latinx students are pouring into the institution but trickling out without a degree in hand. The numbers show that. But when resources get scarce, people start fighting over crumbs, which makes it difficult to address the real issue at hand, which is that students of color are not graduating. People we talked to said that the HSI designation creates further conflict, as people from groups other than Latinx groups may think that they are not benefitting from an institution that seemingly serves one racial group. Does being an HSI mean that we do not serve non-Latinx students? This is an important question for us all to grapple with. We cannot ignore the fact that while being an HSI may be good for all, there is a perception that it is only good for one racialized group. In many ways, this is a false assumption, as we learned that the federal grants that we get benefit all students. But the challenge is that there is a perception that Latinx students are getting more attention and more funding than Black students as a result of being an HSI. Many of the people we spoke to said that we need to do a better job of talking about what it means to be an HSI—and what it doesn't mean. We are not exclusive, but this must be stressed. Bottom line, we can't progress as an institution that supports, validates, and graduates Black and Brown students until the Black and Brown faculty and staff stop fighting these insignificant battles." The crowd cheers again, recognizing the importance of what I have just said.

I continue on. "Challenge number two: We need more Latinx faculty and administrators. This is something nearly every person we talked to stressed. We cannot be a Latinx-serving institution until we address this vital component. Latinx faculty and faculty of color are more likely to understand the needs of students of color and incorporate their ways of knowing into the classroom. Students of color on this campus are having negative experiences with faculty, and many times these experiences are racialized. If students are feeling uncomfortable and unsafe in the classroom, they will not go to office hours, they will not ask faculty for help, and they will not succeed. We talked to students who have had positive experiences, but we cannot ignore the fact that some students do not feel welcome in the classroom, as the classroom is essential to academic success. And we can't rely on faculty in Latino studies, justice studies, women and gender studies, counseling, and social work to do all the work. All departments must make an effort to hire more faculty of color and to require their white faculty to be culturally competent. We have trainings on this campus to become an ally to the LGBT community and the undocumented student community. All faculty should participate in these efforts. And there should be more required trainings for faculty. We learned that a lot of HSIs get grants to provide additional training to faculty.[4]

"We learned that we are making progress toward hiring more faculty of color. For example, while only 10% of those faculty on campus with tenure are Latinx, 16% of all faculty on the tenure track are Latinx. We are also seeing other faculty of color, with only 48% of those faculty members on the tenure track identifying as white. This is significant progress. But of course, it is not happening quickly enough, and it's only happening in some departments. One faculty member told us his department hired two tenure stream people of color in the last four years, one Latina and one Black man of African descent. He was proud of that accomplishment and said that they now offer several courses that are centered on the experiences of people of color, both US born and from the diaspora. But then we talked to another faculty member who told us he is the only Latino among his faculty of twenty-five, both tenure and non-tenure stream. We also learned that part of one of our HSI grants was to infuse the curriculum with Latinx issues by hiring immigration and Latinx specialists, so we hired three professors. Some of the HSI grant was used for faculty startup money in the initial year, and then the following year state funding kicked in, so these positions became line items in the state budget. Again, this goes back to our strengths of recognizing our HSI designation and having administrators who are committed to doing this work.

"We also found that while the number of Latinx faculty may be increasing, there is still a lack of diversity among department chairs and deans. There is also a lack of vice presidents, presidents, and provosts who identify as Latinx, despite the fact that there is a growing number of Latinx people in student services positions and coordinator positions. Latinx people at this institution lack power. Until we hold high-level positions, we will not be able to make decisions that are in the best interest of Latinx students. While we have a vice president of student affairs who identifies as Latino, we have never had a provost or a president who identities as such. In order to progress as an HSI, we must tenure and promote more Latinx faculty into management positions on the academic side and hire more Latinx high-level administrators who are aware of the issues that all minoritized students face." The crowd claps again, suggesting that they agree with this sentiment.

I continue to move through the presentation, realizing that I am running out of time. "Finally—and this will be my last point, I promise—the third challenge we found was that our financial context is messed up." People in the crowd shake their head and sigh, "Uh hmm." "It is difficult to serve any students, not just Latinx students, when we are operating without a state budget. We're a state institution. We haven't received our state allocation, and that makes us all insecure. How can we do what we need to do, which is care for, educate, and train people to work in Chicagoland, if we don't even have support from the state? We have faculty and staff who are forced to take furloughs as a way to prevent eliminating entire positions. How can we recruit more Latinx faculty and staff into this type of environment? Nobody in their right mind wants to work at an institution that is financially struggling.

"Unfortunately, we have political problems at the city and state level. Our mayor, our governor, our city and state officials, they are all corrupt." The crowd sighs with displeasure. "Despite being messed up politically and financially, we have benefitted in at least two ways. As I already mentioned, we have been successful at getting federal grants as a result of being an HSI. Those funds come from the federal government, so that helps us bypass the state. The second way we have benefitted is from the state DREAM Act. Being in a state that not only provides in-state tuition to undocumented immigrants, but also has a scholarship fund for these students, is important. Many of our undocumented students would not be able to attend without the DREAM Act and its monetary award program. I appreciate the state for that. But let me remind you that activists fought for that, too. Latinx people in the state of Illinois have always had to demand fair access to resources. We cannot ever forget that!" The crowd cheers again.

Recommendations for Enacting an HSI Organizational Identity

I come the final slide of my presentation. I state, "We now want to present the recommendations that we have, based on the research we did, before moving into an open forum discussion about what y'all think we should be doing. First recommendation: We must recognize that being an HSI *does not* mean we are exclusionary. It means that while we may center the experiences of Latinx people on this campus, we are not simultaneously rejecting other racial groups. By teaching and learning about the plight and struggle of Latinx people in the United States, we can simultaneously recognize the plight and struggle of other racial groups in this country. By valuing the culture, language, and ways of knowing of Latinx people, through curricular and co-curricular programing, we can value the cultures, languages, and ways of knowing of other people. Being an HSI should mean that we recognize and value the struggles of all racial groups, while simultaneously working to break down the systems that have oppressed us all.

"Second recommendation: We must recognize that racism lives here, despite the fact that we are racially diverse. In recognizing racism, we have to understand how racism manifests on college campuses, because it often manifests in ways that are embedded within the positive things on campus. For example, remember the writing-intensive program that was started with the support of an HSI federal grant? We had a professor who teaches Spanish tell us a story about how that program rejected his proposal to designate his Spanish writing course as 'writing intensive.' He was told that writing intensive courses must be in English. Let me ask you this, How can we progress as an HSI if we reject the language that many of our Latinx students know, value, and use to communicate on a regular basis? An outright rejection of Spanish is a racist, nativist attack on Brown people in this institution and in this country." The crowd erupts in cheers. "We cannot allow racism, nativism, or any form of discrimination and oppression to exist on this campus. As long as it does, we cannot call ourselves an HSI." More cheers from the audience. "We also cannot call ourselves a MSI, because Black students also experience racism and microaggressions on this campus. We must address this, which is going to be a difficult endeavor, but we should do it anyway.

"Third recommendation: We must acknowledge the systemic nature of the problem of educating Latinx people in this city, state, and country. Nearly 80% of Black and Latinx students who start their college careers at ACU must take remedial classes in English or math in their first semester or first year. Why? Because many of them come from the public school system, which might not have prepared them for college. While I don't suggest that we place blame on the public schools, because they are struggling just like we are, with wavering political and economic support from the city and the state, we must recognize that this is our reality. And if we are truly committed to providing access to higher education for the Black and Latinx people in this city, then we have to accept the challenge of educating students who have not been fully prepared for college. How do we do that? We must find ways to scale up the programs that engage high school students earlier in the process.

"We have a lot of small transitional support programs that serve twenty to thirty students. For example, we have a bridge program that allows students to take remedial courses the summer before they matriculate. This is great for those students, but how can we make it so that all students participate? If we know that nearly 80% of first-year students will need developmental classes, why can't we provide them for all students? Since research has shown that transitional programs may not be enough to affect long-term persistence, we must also scale up other support programs on campus that have historically served first-generation, low-income, and/or students of color (Wathington, Pretlow, & Barnett, 2016). These include TRiO programs and programs like

GEAR UP, which helps parents understand the transition to college. We must assume that programs that are good for minoritized students are good for all students, regardless of their background (Garcia & Okhidoi, 2015).

"Fourth recommendation: We must decolonize our institutional structures. We heard a lot of grumbling about tensions between administrators and faculty on this campus. Moving toward a decolonized structure would require us to decentralize decision making in a way that allows individual areas on campus to have autonomy. This would allow individual units to make decisions that are best for their students, without worrying that the administration will eventually reject their approach. This will require us to hire more people of color for faculty and staff positions on campus, which is also essential for decolonizing HSIs. There must be a good mix of people on campus who have various racial, cultural, and indigenous ways of knowing and who can make decisions that are in the best interest of our minoritized student population (Garcia, 2018a). We must then move into evaluating our rewards structure, to make sure that faculty and staff are rewarded for doing work that is anti-racist, anti-nativist, decolonial, and anti-oppressive all together (Garcia, 2018a). Overall, in order to decolonize our structures, we must first recognize that this institution was not founded for indigenous, immigrant, low-income, or minoritized people or for people of color. In doing that, we can then address all the ways in which it operates and approaches education in a Western, white patriarchal way. In doing this, we can disrupt those structures and create a more inclusive environment." The crowd, once again, claps excitedly. A few people whistle. "Thank you all for being patient and listening to this presentation. I want to go ahead an open it up for comments. There are a few of my *colegas* (colleagues) out there with microphones. If you want to speak, please raise your hand, and they will bring you a mic." Hands go up immediately, as Andrea scuttles to get the microphone to the person who raised their hand first.[5] They begin to speak.

Recognizing the Tensions of Embracing an HSI Identity

"Hello. My name is Professor Villanueva. Thank you for your presentation. It was very informative. I think my only comment is about the term, 'Hispanic-Serving Institution.' I don't like the term. A lot of our Latino students do not self-identify as Hispanic. Hispanic is Eurocentric, but most of our Latino students don't have European ancestry. Instead, they might have indigenous or African influences. We have a lot of Puerto Ricans here, so a lot of African influence. We have a lot of Mexican students, so a lot of indigenous influence. To me, the term 'Hispanic' is incredibly problematic. I would rather hear 'Latino-Serving Institution,' but even then I have a problem. I would much rather have a category like 'Minority-Serving Institution' because it's not just about Latinos. It's also about African Americans. It's about immigrants. We have a lot of immigrants from Asia, from Eastern Europe, some from Africa. It's about first generation. It's about social class. Even if you're white, you might be a minority by the fact that you're low income. I prefer something like 'underrepresented' or 'underserved,' which don't sound as good as 'minority,' but there is a problem with the term 'minority,' too, as our students might be the minority in the United States, but they're not a minority on campus. The term, 'Hispanic-serving' needs to be reevaluated."

I acknowledge the comment and agree, "Yes, I agree, the term is problematic. But it's the term that the government uses to designate us. It's like the term 'Hispanic,' right? Some of us don't want to be labeled as 'Hispanic' either. But you raise an interesting point, in that to be 'Hispanic-serving' or 'Latinx-serving' means to serve all types of minoritized students, not just Latinx students. We ought to strive to reach a point where everybody understands that the term in not exclusionary. Thank you. Next comment?" Another person raises their hand.

"*Hola.* My name is Professor X. I have been on this campus for twenty years, and I have been fighting with administrators for twenty years to get them to recognize the HSI designation and what it means. We have had some victories. Thank you for recognizing that those victories were on the backs of Latino activists like myself.[6] When administrators have historically made decisions that did not include us, we have stood up and demanded that they recognize us. We didn't get that new satellite campus because the white administrators wanted to give it to us. We got it because we demanded it, and we got local politicians, foundations, and supporters to help us fight for it. Thank you for recognizing our struggle in your presentation." The audience claps and cheers loudly. One person yells, "*Viva la lucha* (long live the struggle)."

Professor X continues. "One of the concerns I have, which you did not mention, is that we are a Hispanic-Serving Institution because we enroll Latinos at the undergraduate level. But what about at the graduate level? I teach graduate students, and nearly all my students are white. It's disheartening. My biggest concern is that Latino students are not entering graduate programs, which is a problem. They should! We cannot stop Latinos at the undergraduate level. These days it means nothing. We need to encourage our Latino students to move forward to a master's degree because the competition in the job market right now is asking for a master's degree as a minimum requirement. That has to be aligned with whatever classification the institution will have in the future. If we really want to be a HSI, we have to start focusing on graduate-level education as well." Before I can acknowledge the comment, another person stands and starts talking.

"I agree with Professor X's comment about having to fight with administrators in order to be recognized. And while you acknowledged that the administration has been somewhat supportive, I just want to add that the previous president was very pro-Latino and pro-HSI; this president is not. She is pushing her neoliberal education agenda, which quite frankly is harmful to our first-generation, low-income students. How can our students, who are struggling to make ends meet, afford to live on campus in the new fancy residence halls? They can't. But all she cares about is the revenue that can be generated from those residence halls. Her and her administration are essentially catering to rich kids, out-of-state kids, and international students. They're completely out of touch with what our student body is all about. They're searching in Saudi Arabia and other places like that for students instead of focusing on what we do well, which is serving our regional, low-income communities of color. That's what we're all about, and that's what we're good at. That makes us an HSI. The administration thinks that the rich students are going to help the campus become more prestigious and economically stable, particularly because we are operating without a state budget right now. But what do we lose in the process? We lose our ability to effectively serve Latinos, low-income students, and first-generation students from Chicago. There's a disconnect between who we are, at our core, and who we want to be. The faculty believe that we should continue to be who we have always been, which is an institution that caters to and serves the students who come here naturally." The crowd claps as they continue, almost without taking a breath.

"I also think there's a great deal of racism here." The crowd snaps loudly. "We have a real problem on our campus, where almost all of the administration, and especially the high-level administration, is white. I think they literally fear Latino students and Latinos with power, and are therefore reluctant to empower us to hold these types of positions. All they want to do is use us to get federal funding and then disassociate themselves from us as soon as we bring up the issues we are facing. I mean, they profit from the HSI status when they can, but then they ignore us when it's actually time to act on it. I think it's a combination of racism and neoliberalism. They use their white liberal excuses, saying that we want to serve all students, which means that they don't value Latino students as much as they value rich, international students who are willing to pay for tuition and housing and don't ask for much in return. When our Latino students ask for things, like when they asked for a Latino Cultural Center, the administrators refuse, stating that those types of programs are exclusionary. I'm sorry, that is just racist!" The crowd again cheers and chants loudly.

I allow the crowd to quiet down and then thank the professor for their comments. "Thank you for your insight professor, I agree with you. What about students? What do y'all think about us being an HSI, and what we should be doing?" I proceed to look for students who are willing to share. A woman wearing a hijab raises her hand. Andrea passes the microphone to her, and she begins to speak. "Hi, my name is Paige. I am an Arab American; both of my parents are Arab, but I was born here in the United States. I like it at ACU because it is very diverse, and I have noticed that a lot of different groups come together, unlike in high school where there were a lot of cliques. People here are accepting of one another, regardless of race or religion or sexual orientation, and I like that. I don't think that being an HSI is a bad thing. I think we are welcoming and inclusive for Latino people, but we're also welcoming and inclusive of Arab people. But I *would* like us to be an Arab-serving institution, too. For me that would mean having a place where I can pray, because I am Muslim, and I need a space to pray sometimes when I am on campus. That would also mean having more Arab-identified faculty. I don't think that ACU is exclusionary, but there is always more we can do to be more inclusive, right?" The crowd claps in agreement.

Another student raises their hand and begins to speak as Andrea hands them the microphone. "I agree with Paige. This institution is very welcoming. I am American, born here; my family is Swedish, German, and Irish, but I am American and I like the diversity here. I think that being an HSI is like being ADA [Americans with Disabilities Act] approved. It's a seal that it's a good school. It means that it's a good stamp that it's diverse, that you're not going to just get one type of person here. It's a reflection of the city, which is very diverse, too. I like it here." I thank them and ask Andrea to hand the microphone to another student who is raising their hand.

"Hi. I'm Bernadette. I'm a graduate student, and before coming here I went to another institution here in the city that is a Research 1 university, and all they care about is research and publishing. This institution is different. I feel like I belong here because I want to apply what I am learning, which is what this institution is all about. It is important that we recognize what this institution is good at, which is applied learning. But I think we still have a lot of work to do to become an HSI. This institution is more than just Hispanic-serving; it is serving first-generation students, and low-income students, and students who speak Spanish. And we have programs and services for those different populations on this campus, but students are not necessarily aware of them. I just discovered a program on the fourth floor of the library that is for English language learners. I have been here two-and-a-half years but never heard of it. We need to do a better job of promoting the things that make us Hispanic-serving, like special programs and services. The Latino Cultural Center is also an important space on this campus, but it is tucked away in the back of a building that I never even go into. Why? It's a beautiful center, with murals on the walls, and a kitchen, and a place to study or talk to friends. Why isn't it in the middle of campus? Location matters. We all know that. The important programs and services should be more accessible, and we should all know about them. I think we are doing a great job in many ways, especially when compared to my other campus, but I agree with Paige, there is always more we can do."

I thank them for their comments and proceed to wrap up the town hall meeting, as we are running out of time. "Are there any other comments, from faculty or students? We have time for two more comments." Another hand goes up, and Andrea hands the student the microphone. "Hello everybody. I wasn't planning to say anything, but I feel comfortable sharing how I feel about this institution. This is the third school I have been to here in the city, and I just feel most comfortable here. I am mostly Caucasian of European American decent, also mixed with Cuban, but I didn't always feel like I fit in other places where there were mostly Asians and people with blond hair. I don't think of this as a Hispanic-Serving Institution; it's just a place where you feel comfortable no matter who you are. One of my social work professors always talks about Mexicans and Mexican issues, and I think it's interesting, and I learn a lot. But we also talk in our classes about things affecting LGBT people, and I like that too. It's just a place where you can feel comfortable, no matter who you are, and also learn about different cultures. I appreciate that." They hand the microphone back to Andrea and quickly sit down, almost like they are embarrassed.

"Thank you for that. I appreciate your feedback. We have time for one last comment, maybe from someone who has suggestions for how we can do better to serve all students, since y'all seem to suggest that being an HSI means that all students are welcomed here." A hand goes up. Andrea hands them the microphone. "I appreciate all the comments today. Your presentation was eye-opening. And I appreciate all the diverse perspectives. I agree with everybody. I think this is a good place and is doing good things. But I also agree that there is still racism and discrimination here. And the discrimination I see is the discrimination toward nontraditional students. Like, the financial office, why does it close at 4:30 pm? What about students who work all day and can't get here by 4:30 pm? The Latino Cultural Center closes at 5:00 pm. As a result, some students never get to experience that center. We also don't provide child care here on campus. If we really want to cater to all students, including working students and parenting students, who may also be Latino students and Black students, but could be white students too, then we need to address their needs. A parenting student might need child care more than they need a cultural center. Also, why is the coffee shop so expensive?" Someone in the audience yells, "Word," and others clap. "Some of us don't have $3.50 to spend on coffee every day, but we want coffee. Why can't the school provide free coffee? It doesn't have to be gourmet, just no-name coffee and some cream and sugar would be nice. There are small things I think we need to think about in order to be more inclusive. Inclusivity is complex and intersectional." Loud snaps from the crowd.

I thank everyone for their comments as people begin to leave the room. "I realize we are out of time and many of you have other places to be. Please complete an evaluation form and use the blank space to provide more comments. We will compile them and submit them to the administration. Thank you all for coming. *Muchas gracias.*"

A Model of a Latinx-Enhancing Organizational Identity

Two days after the town hall meeting, we meet with our professor, Dr. Bettencourt, to talk about it. As Andrea and I walk into his office, he congratulates us on a successful event and then asks us for our thoughts. Andrea begins, "People seemed to agree on many things, like the fact that we need more faculty of color, and we need to serve more than Latinx students. But there were also strong differences between what the faculty thought and what the students thought. The faculty are more critical, but students seem content with the idea of being an HSI. They just want more basic services, like affordable coffee, which has nothing to do with being an HSI."

Dr. Bettencourt interjects, "But perhaps it has everything to do with being an HSI. As we know, HSIs tend to enroll low-income students, which means that students at an HSI probably do care about affordable amenities and services on campus. The identities of Latinx students are so complex that it seems that an HSI organizational identity is also complex, right? Perhaps HSIs have intersectional identities, just like Latinx students. This seemed to come out during the town hall meeting; HSIs should be more than Latinx-serving; they should be low-income student–serving, immigrant student–serving, students with disabilities–serving, international student–serving, first-generation student–serving, parenting student–serving. We could go on and on. For us, being an HSI means accepting, validating, and supporting students from many minoritized, intersectional identities." We all consider this comment for a moment, quietly in our own thoughts.

Dr. Bettencourt continues. "The strengths that you all presented are important. You argued that ACU has historically been an HSI because of the programs, services, and curriculum that we offer. Coming from several other institutions that did not have any of the resources or academic programs for Latinx students that we do, I would have to agree. There is something important about those historical elements that have become embedded within the intuition. There are clear cultural indicators, or distinct assumptions, beliefs, and values, about how we serve Latinx students (Garcia, 2017). Latinx students have the opportunity to learn about who they are as racialized, colonized people in the United States. They can take classes that teach them about the struggles that Latinx students face in the educational system; they can take classes that teach them about how the criminal justice system discriminates against them; and they can take classes that teach them how to support immigrant populations in their home communities. And although it seems like some students are not aware of the support programs on campus, the programs are available. Validating students' racial, ethnic, and cultural ways of knowing is an important indicator of serving them, right?"

I jump in. "Yes, but what about the tensions that we noted about racism and microaggressions? Some students told us that they have heard faculty members make comments that are offensive in class. One student told us that a faculty member said that students shouldn't come here until they can pass basic math and English, because it is a waste of our time and resources to remediate students. That student had to take three developmental classes here and felt ashamed after hearing that. Faculty who work here need to understand that this isn't Harvard, and our students have struggled, like real-life struggles—struggles they can't imagine. Some students have seen friends get shot and family members deported or taken to jail. They have experienced trauma. I appreciate that ACU admits students who are not the top of their class, and we have to do better to make them feel like they belong here once they get here. To be Hispanic-serving means to be welcoming to all students, regardless of experiences and academic abilities. We have to accept students for who they are and then help them to become productive citizens who give back to the disadvantaged communities that they come from. Being from the 'hood is not a deficit, it's an asset. Our students come here, take classes with people like you, Dr. Bettencourt, who come from their same 'hood and who teach them how to go out and work for the betterment of their communities. That's what being an HSI is, in my opinion."

Dr. Bettencourt agrees and begins writing on the dry-erase board in his office. He goes into professor mode and draws several empty boxes on the board. He then asks us, "Based on the research that you did and the information collected at the town hall meeting, what elements are most essential for us becoming an institution that recognizes and validates

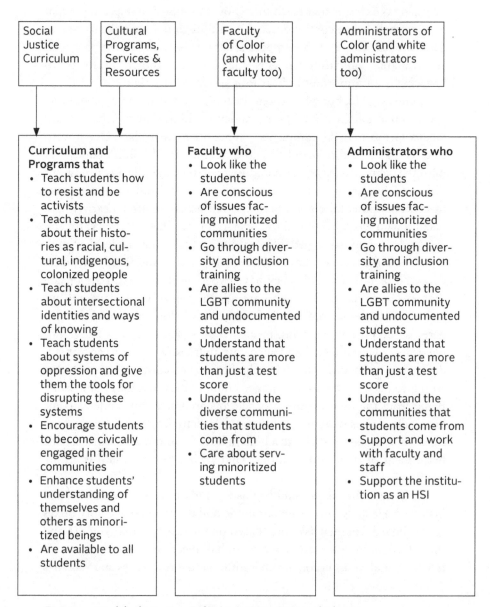

Figure 2. Preliminary Model of a Latinx-Enhancing Organizational Identity.

| Social Justice Curriculum | Cultural Programs, Services & Resources | Faculty of Color (and white faculty too) | Administrators of Color (and white administrators too) |

Curriculum and Programs that
- Teach students how to resist and be activists
- Teach students about their histories as racial, cultural, indigenous, colonized people
- Teach students about intersectional identities and ways of knowing
- Teach students about systems of oppression and give them the tools for disrupting these systems
- Encourage students to become civically engaged in their communities
- Enhance students' understanding of themselves and others as minoritized beings
- Are available to all students

Faculty who
- Look like the students
- Are conscious of issues facing minoritized communities
- Go through diversity and inclusion training
- Are allies to the LGBT community and undocumented students
- Understand that students are more than just a test score
- Understand the diverse communities that students come from
- Care about serving minoritized students

Administrators who
- Look like the students
- Are conscious of issues facing minoritized communities
- Go through diversity and inclusion training
- Are allies to the LGBT community and undocumented students
- Understand that students are more than just a test score
- Understand the communities that students come from
- Support and work with faculty and staff
- Support the institution as an HSI

Figure 3. Model of a Latinx-Enhancing Organizational Identity.

Latinx students for who they are and where they have come from? And even further, an institution that embraces an intersectional identity, or one that serves students that have many intersecting identities?" I look at the boxes and begin to think. Andrea approaches the board first and writes a few words.

I agree with the elements Andrea has added to the boxes, but I think that they are too basic. We need to be more specific about what these things mean. I draw a line from each box and add on.

We all look at the board, content with this model for enhancing the cultural and racial experience of Latinx and other minoritized students. I take a picture of it and agree to type it up to include with our report to the administration. We are hopeful about our institution's progress as an HSI, but we know there is still work to be done in order to fully become Latinx-serving.

FOUR

Serving the Latinx Community in the Third Space

THE LATINX population is one of the largest racialized groups in the United States, with 56.6 million people identifying as Latinx in 2015, or 17.6% of the population (US Census Bureau, 2016). This representation is rapidly increasing, with predictions that the Latinx population will reach 119 million by 2060, or 29% of the population (Colby & Ortman, 2014). This population increase is simultaneously reflected in postsecondary enrollment. In fall 2015, three million of the 17 million students enrolled in undergraduate programs in the United States self-identified as Latinx, which is 17.6% of the total undergraduate population, making them the second largest racialized group in higher education, behind white students (National Center for Education Statistics, 2017). Despite the growing presence of Latinxs in higher education, their postsecondary completion rates are inequitable compared to their white counterparts (NCES, 2017). They are also more likely than white students to enroll in less selective, broad-access institutions, including community colleges, where, for a number of reasons, their chances of completing a degree program are lower (Carnevale & Strohl, 2013; Flores & Park, 2013).

In 1992, the federal government formally recognized broad-access institutions that enroll a large percentage of Latinx as Hispanic-Serving Institutions with the specific role of providing access to higher education.

In many ways, the federal designation legitimized HSIs, although these institutions had been actively advocating for Latinx students and providing them with an opportunity to enter postsecondary education for nearly thirty years (Laden, 2001, 2004). The expansion of HSIs in the 1970s and 1980s was fueled by the civil rights movement of the 1960s, when postsecondary institutions were challenged to open their doors to Black and Latinx students (Laden, 2001; MacDonald et al., 2007; Olivas, 1982). Responding to student demands and pressures from such external organizations as the Hispanic Association of Colleges and Universities and the President's Advisory Commission on Educational Excellence for Hispanic Americans, formerly white institutions became racially minoritized. The racialization of postsecondary institutions, while complex, created a pathway to postsecondary education for Latinx people, a racialized group that has historically been on the margins in all aspects of education.

Committing to Access

For HSIs, the commitment to access extends beyond the Latinx community to other minoritized groups that are often subjugated and deemed "undesirable" (based on race, immigration status, native language, etc.) in most elite (white) institutions. For example, they enroll a large percentage of Black and Asian American students, low-income students, non-native English speakers, immigrant students, students who are academically underprepared, and students who attended high schools with a high concentration of racially minoritized students (Contreras et al., 2008; Flores & Park, 2015; Núñez & Bowers, 2011). Both two- and four-year HSIs enroll students who attended high schools with few resources, such as guidance counselors who support students' aspirations of attending college and workshops that help students with the college application process and test preparation (Núñez & Bowers, 2011). Flores and Park (2015) also found that Latinx students who enroll in HSIs in Texas took fewer advanced placement mathematics courses in high school than did those who attend non-HSIs. HSIs are essential to increasing the postsecondary participation of students living on the margins of a highly racialized society.

Providing access to minoritized people, therefore, is a central and distinct aspect of the organizational identity of HSIs (Garcia, 2016), with individual case studies revealing this commitment. In the 1980s, the University of Texas at San Antonio (UTSA) took active steps to increase the enrollment of students of color by opening a downtown campus and developing provisional admission programs (Doran, 2015). The president of UTSA and the mayor of San Antonio were committed to access, as reflected in the admission policies and in their opening a campus that was more accessible to people of color. In assessing the "institutional readiness" of postsecondary institutions located in Latinx enclaves (those with a growing population of Latinxs), Torres and Zerquera (2012) found that out of the nineteen institutions they examined, five were committed to becoming HSIs. They defined "committed" as being aware of the changing demographics of the region, clearly defining institutional diversity, making efforts to meet the needs of the regional Latinx community, and emphasizing a supportive campus climate for Latinxs (Torres & Zerquera, 2012). Garcia (2016) reported that one HSI in the Southwest made formal claims about their commitment to serving the region, which had a 42% Latinx population, as reflected in their long-term implementation of outreach and recruitment to low-income students, first-generation students, and students of color. While these examples have limited generalizability, they suggest that some HSIs are in fact committed to providing access to minoritized students and actively seeking to do so, rather than accidentally becoming HSIs.

Embracing Language/Bilingualism

Being committed to access, however, is simply not enough to be considered a Latinx-serving institution. Moving from simply enrolling Latinx students to effectively serving them requires an institution to recognize, embrace, and enhance the racial and cultural ways of knowing of Latinx students (Garcia, 2017). For Latinx students in postsecondary education, this includes a recognition of the Spanish language. As noted by Anzaldúa (1987), "Ethnic identity is twin skin to linguistic identity—I am my language. Until I can take pride in my language, I cannot take pride in myself" (p. 81). With more than 37 million Spanish speakers in the United States (Lopez & Gonzalez-Barrera, 2013), recognizing and valuing the Spanish language as a legitimate language of communication in educational settings is becoming essential. Although research suggests that students who attend HSIs feel comfortable speaking Spanish with their peers, faculty, and administrators (Dayton, Gonzalez-Vasquez, Martinez, & Plum, 2004; Guardia & Evans, 2008; Sebanc, Hernandez, & Alvarado, 2009), these interactions are informal and not necessarily legitimized at the institutional level. What then would it look like for an entire organization to enact an identity for serving *linguistically* diverse students? Even further, what would it look like for HSIs to not only embrace the language of many of their students, but simultaneously enhance it? These questions are difficult to answer, as very few US postsecondary institutions are founded as bilingual institutions. It's challenging to imagine what this type of space would look like because there are very few models.

Moreover, while language can bind the Latinx community, it can also divide it if the language diversity within the group is not considered, as Latinxs fall along a language continuum, from English dominant to Spanish only, with a range of language abilities between these two extremes. Even at postsecondary institutions such as the University of Texas–Pan American (UTPA), which is located twenty minutes from the US–Mexico border and enrolls over 85% Latinx students, it is inaccurate to assume that most students speak Spanish (Méndez Newman, 2007; Ramírez-Dhoore & Jones, 2007). Furthermore, there is some level of "linguistic shaming" toward those who do not speak Spanish (Ramírez-Dhoore & Jones, 2007). Yet in shaming people for their linguistic (in)abilities, it is forgotten that Latinxs are a colonized people, stripped of their indigenous language and forced to speak the colonizer's tongue (Anzaldúa, 1987). As such, the entire Latinx community has been exposed to "linguistic terrorism" (Anzaldúa, 1987). Institutions, therefore, must be careful not to reiterate this "terrorism." Moreover, Méndez Newman (2007) argues that institutions must avoid the "English as a second language" label, as it is deficit-based, reductive, and colonial, implying that students are linguistic and cultural foreigners.

Recognizing the complexities of embracing and enhancing the language skills of Latinxs, HSIs should nonetheless move toward legitimizing language diversity among Latinx students, which will ultimately translate into effectively serving them. A number of case studies reflect these efforts at several HSIs. Understanding the long history of the educational system's racist attempts to rid Latinx students of the Spanish language (Anzaldúa, 1987; G. G. González, 2008; MacDonald, 2004), faculty at UTPA have altered their pedagogy so that it is responsive to the language needs of Latinx students. UTPA professors Dora Ramírez-Dhoore and Rebecca Jones recognize that Latinx and Spanish-speaking students may respond differently to a variety of teaching styles, including those that are normative in educational settings, and they acknowledge that "particular things within a political and educational space necessitate differences in practice and theory" (Ramírez-Dhoore & Jones, 2007, p. 68). This is essential, as HSIs are geographically located in regions that have very unique political and educational contexts that must be considered in order to effectively serve students.

Through personal narratives reflective of their own experiences teaching writing composition with linguistically diverse Latinxs at UTPA, Ramírez-Dhoore and Jones (2007) highlight the inherent struggle of implementing the "proper pedagogy" for this group of students while trying to "[think] through the third spaces, [resist] the dichotomies, and [avoid] the 'linguistic terrorism'" (p. 79). Faculty teaching racially and linguistically minoritized students must find a balance between helping students to understand and master academic discourse, which is the colonizer's discourse, while simultaneously resisting it (Ramírez-Dhoore & Jones, 2007). This is the challenge for faculty at HSIs who want to be culturally responsive in their teaching approach yet recognize that in the United States, white discourses are usually the only legitimate ones. Students also recognize this need to speak and write in legitimized ways, and they too want to master the dominant narrative of their fields in order to be successful (Ramírez-Dhoore & Jones, 2007).

In Florida, faculty teaching at the University of Miami (an emerging HSI) have also considered what it means to teach linguistically diverse students. University of Miami professors Isis Artze-Vega, Elizabeth Doud, and Belkys Torres argue that writing composition courses are ideal for infusing bilingualism, as the fundamental skills taught, such as "critical thinking, assignment compliance, audience awareness, and providing evidence, clarity, and organization—indisputably transcend languages" (Artze-Vega, Doud, & Torres, 2007, p. 100). They note, however, that bilingualism at the postsecondary level looks different than at the primary and secondary level, as most US institutions of higher education require students to be competent in English. They suggest that a proper approach to bilingualism in higher education may be "maintenance," meaning it should "conserve both languages being used, and trust that this approach will enhance students' academic achievement" (Artze-Vega et al., 2007, p. 100).

Like Professors Ramírez-Dhoore and Jones at UTPA, Professors Artze-Vega, Doud, and Torres are actively trying to find the "proper pedagogy" for teaching bilingual composition, acknowledging that there are few models at the postsecondary level, while drawing on the extensive knowledge at the primary and secondary level. They urge bilingual composition teachers to experiment with various options, such as using both languages concurrently in class or switching between languages, depending on the topic. They also suggest that faculty utilize Spanish, English, and bilingual texts, and stress the importance of allowing students to choose which language they will use when they submit their assignments, while being open to the use of both simultaneously (Artze-Vega et al., 2007).

Teaching bilingual courses at HSIs is an effective way to increase the level of "servingness" at these institutions, but there are limits to this approach, as evidenced by the diversity of linguistic abilities, not only among students, but also among the faculty at these institutions. Bilingual courses also have their limits when it comes to institutional implications. If only a small segment of the teaching population at an HSI, or any postsecondary institution, has the ability and desire to convert their classrooms into bilingual spaces, the organization will not likely be transformed. What then does it look like for an entire institution to be transformed into what Gutiérrez, Rymes, and Larson (1995) call a "third space"?

Defining the Third Space

The third space is "the social space within which counter-hegemonic activity or contestation of dominant discourses can occur for both students and teachers," where the "*how* of both social and critical theory can be implemented" (Gutiérrez et al., 1995, p. 451). It is within the third space that competing discourses and epistemologies exist—a place where multiple world views collide and new scripts simultaneously develop (Gutiérrez et al., 1995). Power and authority must be reconsidered within the third space, and dominant cultural values and ways of knowing must be flexible, allowing for the emergence of minoritized perspectives. There is tension in this process, as is to be expected when official learning spaces collide with unofficial learning spaces; yet this conflict is the catalyst for expanded learning within the third space (Gutiérrez, Baquedano-López, & Tejeda, 1999). This expanded learning emerges as a result of "a transformative space where the potential for an expanded form of learning and the development of new knowledge are heightened" (Gutiérrez, 2008).

While the third space has largely been conceptualized at the classroom level in primary and secondary schools, here I hypothesize what it would look at the organizational level in a postsecondary setting. This argument is grounded in challenging the dominant values of postsecondary education, which are historically aligned with all things white. From the dominant perspective, the whiter an institution is, the better it is in comparison to normative standards such as selectivity, prestige, research dollars, and talent of faculty and students (as measured subjectively). The value placed on white institutions is the natural outcome of the racialization process. HSIs are actively challenging these expectations.

Amarillo Private College as a Third Space

This counterstory is about Amarillo Private College, which was founded as and is centered on being a bilingual institution, yet recognizes that there are limits to serving linguistically diverse students. Its core mission is to enroll and serve the Latinx community in Chicagoland. The story is a composite, grounded in the data collected, but also informed by the scant literature on bilingualism in postsecondary education, theoretical ideologies about the third space, and my own experiences (Solórzano & Yosso, 2002). Data for this counterstory include one-on-one interviews with faculty and staff at APC, historical documents about the institution, reports published by the institution, a review of APC's website, and ethnographic observations at three of the five satellite campuses.

This counterstory conceptualizes a Latinx-serving organizational identity in which students succeed according to dominant, white normative standards (i.e., they graduate and get jobs) while also experiencing a more transformative experience that recognizes and validates their cultural and linguistic ways of knowing (Garcia, 2017). This counterstory is narrated by Nayeli, a reporter who writes for a small Chicago-based monthly newspaper. Her editor asked her to write for a special section of the next issue, focusing on postsecondary institutions in the city. The newspaper is committed to keeping local residents informed about political, educational, and economic issues facing their communities. Illinois has been dealing with a state budget crisis because legislators have refused to pass a budget for the last two fiscal years. Nayeli and her editor felt a special section focusing on colleges and universities would be appropriate, as both public and private institutions are affected by the state budget. They decided the special section would highlight four unique types of institutions in the city, including HSIs, predominantly Black institutions, Asian American and Native American Pacific Islander–Serving Institutions (AANAPISIs), and historically white institutions.

Nayeli chose one institution of each type for her story, including APC. She felt this was a good opportunity to highlight an institution founded to serve the Latinx community in Chicagoland. As a graduate of a historically white, highly selective institution in the city, she did not know much about APC and did not know anyone who had attended it. In reflecting on her own college-going process, she remembered that no one ever talked about APC at her Chicago Public Schools magnet school. The push was always to attend the University of Illinois, University of Chicago, Loyola University Chicago, or DePaul University. She now realizes how elitist this was. Through her research on APC, she found that it serves a specific purpose, very different from the elite colleges and universities she was exposed to in high school. APC provides access for post-traditional students, including older, returning, and parenting students; students who did not attend magnet schools; students who may not see themselves as college-going material; and students who want to learn English. She secured an interview with an administrator who had been at the institution for nearly thirty years and was excited to talk to him to learn more about this unique mission.

The Interviews

Tuesday morning. I literally run into the office at 8:56 am, coffee in hand, trying not to trip in my four-inch heels. My phone interview is scheduled for 9:00 am, and I don't want to be late. I drop my shoulder bag on the chair, place my coffee on the desk, trying not to spill it, and pick up the phone to dial. The phone rings twice before a man answers,

"Hello." I am relieved to hear his voice and say, "*Buenos dias, Señor,* this is Nayeli, how are you this morning?" "Oh, Nayeli, hello, I'm doing well, *muy bien*, thanks." I smile and reply, "Great. Thank you again for agreeing to speak with me this morning." He responds, "No problem. I am happy to talk to you." I proceed: "As I mentioned to you in my email, I am writing a story about four colleges and universities in the city for a special section of next month's issue of our paper. We are featuring a story on APC, with its unique history of serving the Latinx community in Chicagoland. But as I did my research on APC, I found that few people I talked to are aware of APC. Why aren't more people in the area aware of your college and the wonderful work that you are doing with the Latino community?"

He quickly answers, "That's a great question. I think the bottom line is that we're a no-frills institution with a very specific mission. We're an institution that was created for the purpose of serving the Latino community in Chicagoland by providing access to quality, affordable education. We are also an example of what higher education can look like in an urban setting, at an institution that functions with far more limited resources than other institutions. But we believe that everybody should have access to higher education. We believe in the value of education as a transformation tool for the Latino community. We also believe in the value of being bilingual in today's society. And overall, we believe in assuring that all students are able to fulfill their dreams. Why don't more people know about us? Probably because we're not a big university; we don't do research; we don't develop cures for diseases; we don't get grants from the National Science Foundation; we don't have a Division I football team; we don't have a campus with buildings that were built over 100 years ago; we're not a top ranked university in *U.S. News and World Reports*. Basically, we aren't a traditional institution."

I quickly add my two cents. "You mean you're not a white institution, because those are things that white institutions do." He laughs, "That's true. We sort of fly under the radar in the mainstream world. We advertise on Spanish radio stations, and we do a lot of outreach in predominantly Latino, Spanish-speaking communities. The white people probably don't care much about the work that we're doing, and that's okay with us, because we don't care what they are doing, either." We both laugh.

I continue, "Your main focus is to provide the Latino community with access to higher education. Can you tell me more about that? What does that look like?" He pauses only momentarily before stating, "It's hard to explain what that looks like because, as a college, during our daily life, we often don't think much about it. We just try to operate. Perhaps I'm exaggerating a little, but we were created with the purpose of serving the Latino community, by providing access to higher education to the population. Anyone who has the ability to benefit from our programs can be admitted. We keep the costs low so that anybody, no matter what their income is, can attend. Also, what is very important to our community here is that we have a bilingual program, so that immigrant students, who make up about half our student population, can take content classes in their native language, Spanish. Psychology 101, American history, literature, a variety of classes are offered in Spanish. They can earn credit at the same time that they are progressing with their English. The bilingual program represents a core value when we think about who we are."

"Thank you for that clarification," I reply. "It helps me to understand a little more about how you define 'access.' There are two things that you said that I want to ask you more about. The first is that you have a bilingual program. Can you tell me more about what that looks like, as it is a unique model for higher education?" He quickly jumps in, "Yes, offering bilingual education makes us very unique. We're a bilingual institution. Most of the staff speak Spanish, we offer classes in Spanish, and we are culturally sensitive to the Hispanic population. For example, for many students who come to our institution, their level of English is not extensive enough to take advanced courses in the subject of their career in English. We allow them to take a lower-level content course in Spanish while they are learning English. Those classes count toward their degree, so they are not wasting time. Once they have completed their basic English classes, they can transfer into their degree program and transition to courses that are all in English. The idea is to help people preserve their culture, traditions, and language, while providing them with the tools to work in the United States, which requires English. In this way, the institution is transformational; we transform people's lives by recognizing that language is not a deficit. We actually think being monolingual is a deficit." We both laugh.

He continues, "The research on bilingual education would suggest that our students are smarter when they graduate because they can function in at least two languages. By *function*, I mean that we teach them the vocabulary of their field in both languages. Even students who come into the institution already bilingual typically only know how to communicate with their Spanish-speaking parents and family members; they don't always know how to communicate with people in their chosen field. We help with that too. While our specialty is transitional bilingual education, meaning our primary goal is to help non-English speakers learn English, we are able to enhance the language skills of all students who come here." I interrupt, "That's great. Do you have a journalism program? Because I could use some help communicating in my field in Spanish." He chuckles, "No, not yet, but we may add one. We are adding a lot of academic programs. I'll keep that one in mind." I quietly reflect on how completely inadequate I am in communicating in Spanish beyond a conversational level.

I shift to another topic. "The second thing I wanted to follow up on was the affordability piece. You have stressed that you provide a quality, affordable education. Can you tell me more about that?" Before I can even finish my question, he begins, "We very much believe that we are providing a service to the Latino population, so we have to try to provide as low cost an education as possible while still maintaining the quality, which means that it is accredited by the Higher Learning Commission here in the Midwest, that we keep in good standing with all the programs and articulations with other institutions and the Illinois Board of Higher Education, and that we maintain the recognized quality standards. Quality is important to us. But affordability is essential. If we cannot provide an affordable education, we won't be able to attract the students whom we care the most about. We do this through state-funded programs, such as the MAP [Monetary Award Program] Award. We also rely on the federal Pell Grant program, as many of our students are low income. We also offer some institutional aid through discounts and donations. We create financial aid packages in which the great majority of our students don't pay anything and have no loan debt. The packages are entirely based on grants and scholarships.

"That's hard to do, but like I said, we're very much a no-frills institution. We don't offer a lot of services and programs to students. Our mentality is that we're serving an adult, nontraditional population, where people just come to class and go home. Our facilities are pretty sparse. We don't have sports. We don't have dorms. We don't have any of those things. We have classrooms, labs, and a few offices. We keep costs low. We also keep costs low by having very few administration staff members and a limited number of full-time faculty; instead, we use mostly adjunct faculty. Finally, every cost has to be examined over and over before an expenditure is made in any area." I jump in, "That's amazing. A lot of institutions could learn from y'all. It seems like common sense, that postsecondary institutions only need the basics, like classrooms, faculty, and key staff members." He adds, "Keeping our expenditures low is essential. But financial aid programs are also essential, and they are the most in danger right now. The Pell Grant program and MAP have not grown in the past six to eight years. It's getting harder and harder to rely on the state and the federal government, which means our students will have to pay out of pocket. We are very reluctant to participate in student loan programs. But if we do, we would keep students' debts very low. We would never graduate anybody with a bachelor's degree and more than $5,000 or $6,000 in debt. It's just not ethical, and we won't do it."

There is a brief pause as I wait to see if he has anything else to add. I then continue, "That makes sense. That's great. Students should get a quality education at an affordable price. But you're right, it is getting harder and harder to provide financial support for students. We are entering our third fiscal year with no state budget, and the federal government seems to be cutting programs for low-income and first-generation students." He replies, "Yes, it's very disappointing. The state budget situation is affecting us all, even private colleges, particularly those that enroll low-income students who need the state support."

I look down at my notes. "Thank you for sharing your thoughts on this, as the state budget crisis was the motivating force behind this story. One additional thing you mentioned was transformation—that you see education as a transformational tool for the Latino community. Can you talk more about that?"

"Yes, of course. We talk about that all the time. For us, it means helping Latinos value their own culture and value the capital that they bring with them, both to campus and to their jobs. We don't believe that Latinos are just unfortunate people who need help. We actually see our students as strong contributors of knowledge. They come here with their own strengths and have something to offer. They belong in higher education; they belong here because they're smart. We see transformation as giving them the tools to go back into their communities and make a difference because they have the culture and they have the language to build their own communities. That means that they are better qualified to serve the Latino communities that they have grown up in or moved to, which includes a lot of areas in Chicago. They have the knowledge, the culture, and the ability to engage with people so that their communities can improve. Some of our students go back to their country of origin and are working there. But for the most part, our students, although they may have come from another country, are settled in the United States at this point. They are transforming our neighborhoods here in Chicago and the state of Illinois as a whole. Whether they are new immigrants or their families have been here for generations, they are committed to their communities here in the region, and we are committed to providing them with the tools to be transformative agents of change in those communities. That's what we mean by transformational tools."

9:25 am. I move to wrap up the interview and thank him for his time. "*Pues*, I know you have another appointment. Before we hang up, do you have anything else you would like to add, with the remaining few minutes we have?" He pauses momentarily. "No, I think that is it for now." I say, "The information you have shared will help me write my story and will help me highlight some of the great things your institution is doing, particularly in working with the Latino community here in Chicago." He bids me farewell and hangs up. I am more excited about this story than I was thirty minutes ago. I imagine what it would be like if all colleges and universities were so dedicated to the advancement of minoritized communities. Society as a whole would benefit from this type of approach, with colleges operating outside the white hegemonic expectations laid out for postsecondary institutions.

* * *

Friday morning. I finally heard back from a professor at APC who is willing to talk to me. I agreed to meet her at 10:30 am at the main campus, which is one of four campuses in the city. I exit the train station and walk down the stairs. I check my map app for directions to the campus and see that it is less than one block from the station. I walk through what appears to be an Asian ethnic enclave, one that I have never ventured through in the past. I continue walking into a residential neighborhood, taking note of the various houses, including brick courtyard-style buildings and two-story flats typical of Chicago. I see the college from a distance—a series of connected, two-story brick buildings with a small APC banner on the building. The college blends in with the neighborhood, nothing pretentious about it. As I walk down the main driveway, I notice an inscription on a building, "Pioneer in Bilingualism." It's fairly quiet as I enter the building, perhaps because it's Friday morning. I am early, so I walk through the main corridor. On one bulletin board, I see a picture of thirteen people with the words "Congrats Grads" on it. I see Latino art, motivational quotes, flyers in both English and Spanish—and some strictly in Spanish. One flyer is for a "Bring a Friend" campus recruitment campaign, and I wonder if that works. Do people bring friends to APC?

I walk into the main administration area where I am greeted in Spanish and asked whether I need help. I tell the woman sitting at the receptionist desk that I am meeting Professor Velez in the library. She points me to the second floor of the building. I walk into the library and see a woman sitting at a table, quietly working on her laptop. I approach her. "Profesora Velez?" She looks up and smiles. "Please, call me Esmeralda," she says, as she rises to greet me. I reach out my hand to shake hers, but instead she opens her arms and embraces me with a hug and a kiss on the cheek. I feel slightly uncomfortable, as it is not common practice to hug a source. Yet I embrace her back, recognizing that the greeting is cultural. "Thank you so much for agreeing to meet with me. I understand you are very busy. I won't keep you too long. I just wanted to ask you a few questions, to help me finalize my story on APC." She quickly says, "No problem. I am happy to help. *Pero*, before we start, *quires café?* (Do you want coffee?)" "No, thank you, I'm fine for now." She smiles and sips on her tea. I ask my first question, "From what I have learned, APC's core mission is to serve as a point of access for the Latino community in Chicago. Can you talk a little bit about this mission and what it means to you?"

"You're exactly right," Professor Velez replies. "We're a private, nonprofit organization with a mission to provide access to the Latino community. The institution actually started that way. It's a very mission-driven institution, and we as faculty are very committed to the mission. We come here knowing that the institution doesn't necessarily have the same resources of larger research institutions, but we have students who want to build a better future for themselves, their families, and their communities. We serve as a bridge to higher education for people who wouldn't otherwise have access to it. The classes are the same classes that you could get somewhere else in terms of the title that you're working with, for example, Psychology 101. It's just the language that they're offered in that makes a significant impact on the Latino community, because we offer the courses in Spanish. I feel like the curriculum isn't different from other colleges or universities in the city, but the language makes it more accessible for the students who come here. Also, our location, I assume, makes us accessible because four of our five campuses are located in heavily Hispanic communities. Location makes a big impact on being able to access the school. I think those things matter."

I agree. "Yes, exactly, those things absolutely matter. One thing I don't have a strong understanding of is what the classroom experience looks like. I have learned that y'all offer courses in Spanish, but as a professor teaching these courses, can you tell me what it actually looks like to be in these classes?" She smiles enthusiastically. "In our classroom—even in the upper-level, junior/senior classrooms, which is what I teach in—I want our students to use both languages in class. I want them to know that both languages are valuable. I may teach the course in English, but the discussion may sometimes be in Spanglish—sometimes it's in English, sometimes it's in Spanish. Most often the discussions are in English because the students are continuing to work at being more fluent themselves. Most of them have made a fantastic start in that. But occasionally they get stuck when trying to express something that's very personal, and Spanish is their first language. What we always say in my program is, 'Say it in Spanish. We'll figure it out.'" We both laugh, and Professor Velez continues. "Some things can't be translated into English, if they're close to the heart and what people are trying to express. Both languages are encouraged and valued—not just encouraged, but also valued. And the students are recognizing that Spanish will be useful to them in their career. It's actually social capital for them. It's something we want them to be clear about. Knowledge of their own culture—we want them to be clear about the value of that. In my program, some of the faculty are not Spanish speakers, and they value and appreciate our students' language and culture as well. I truly believe that. I have never felt otherwise from my non-Latino, non-Spanish-speaking colleagues. Like I said, we all believe in the mission."

I nod in agreement. "There seems to be a focus on career development, and general skill development that will help students in their careers. Can you talk about that? Is that part of the core mission?" Professor Velez stops to think for a moment. "Well, yes. We want students to find better jobs after they graduate. And they do. Almost all of our students work while going to school, and I would say that they are able to find better work after they finish their degrees. Better in terms of the salary; better in terms of satisfaction at their workplace. If this happens, then I think they are successful, and, ultimately, we have succeeded in our mission. If the students improve their lifestyle, if the students find a better job, if the students' salaries are improved, I think we can call that a successful outcome. But also, we want to see students go beyond their associate's degree and complete a bachelor's degree. Because we don't offer extensive bachelor's degree programs, a lot of our students graduate with an associate's degree and get better jobs, and that's fine. But we want them to go on, maybe transfer to other schools in the city. Keep going. We help them to see that education is possible. They can do it. They can succeed. Even if they thought they couldn't, we help them see that they can.

"Also, we want students to get involved in their communities. We have some service-learning courses. We partner with the Latino community to engage students in doing community-based participatory research. Then, when students finish their research project, members of the agency come into the classroom and hear the students' presentations about the research that they did. There's back-and-forth movement between the community and the school built into the curriculum. When students do their internships, most of the time, those internships are in agencies that are serving some part of the Latino population. We encourage community involvement while students are enrolled, and we hope that they continue that involvement when they graduate."

I smile and nod. "Thank you. That helps me to see the value of an education, beyond the direct measurable outcomes typically used by politicians and legislators, like graduation. It's almost like y'all assume students will graduate. You expect it. Instead you focus on other things, less tangible things, like engagement in the community. Is that accurate?"

She smiles back at me. "Yes, *mija*, that's exactly it." The term of endearment she uses, *mija*, makes me feel connected to her. Like she believes in me and wants me to be successful. I imagine what it must be like to attend this institution. I don't think I've ever been in an educational setting where the teachers see me for who I am. But suddenly I feel more visible than I ever have. In the back of my mind I make a note to myself, "You must look into the programs at this school and consider getting another degree." This feeling I have prompts my next question. "Another unmeasurable outcome that many colleges and universities struggle with is sense of belonging. Latino students don't necessarily feel like they belong at many colleges and universities. But that doesn't seem to be the case here. How do you create a sense of belonging for students?"

"I know that is an issue in other places," she agrees. "One of our graduates just went to a very well-known psychology program for her master's degree. Her first year there, she was the valedictorian. But she came back and talked to me, and she was totally depressed. Horrified. She had been made fun of in class because she had an accent. She had a teacher at that institution, and they're supposed to be competent in diversity, but one of the teachers there had told her she didn't belong in their psychology program. I talked with her and tried to empower her to find some other minority students there. Connect with them. Find just one teacher who would listen. Long story short, she did. This was a number of years ago now. She finally got the support she needed, but it took a long time. She was very discouraged, but she didn't want to quit. She's not one to give up. She recently graduated with her master's and is on her way to getting a doctorate there. She has gotten all kinds of awards from them. But other institutions are just not as welcoming, I think, and people don't feel at home.

"Our students sometimes get frustrated because we are demanding. They'll get frustrated and say, 'I'm going to go to the university down the street, it's Hispanic-serving as well.' Fine. They go. They come back, because they don't feel like they have advocates who help them through the system, that help them manage registration in a large place. They get to the door and find out that the course is full, and nobody told them. Just a lot of little things like that. When students come back after graduating from here, they tell us that they felt very well-prepared to go to graduate school. The one psychology student was an outlier. About 20% of our students apply to grad school, and they are graduating.

They're saying that they felt that we prepared them and, in fact, that college was harder for them than grad school. We're pretty demanding. We're not lowering the bar; we're raising it by believing in them and pushing them."

"That's a great example, thank you for sharing. The term 'advocacy' also comes to mind. What does advocacy look like on campus?" She smiles again. "Yes! We are advocates. All of us! The faculty advocate for students, to make things more accessible to them, such as having access to computer labs, making sure their books are in—little things that may seem minute but they're a big part of ensuring that the students receive the help that they need or have access to the things that they need. Staff members are also very vocal in meetings. We have meetings with administrators to check in, get updates, and hear from everybody on how students are doing. I think that's where you see the advocates constantly making sure that we're addressing the needs of the students and finding out in what areas we're lacking. At those meetings, there is typically a Q&A, and that is where you'll have most of the faculty, the advisors, the financial aid counselors, and people from different departments who will bring up a point, like we're having this issue with students. We all work together to solve it, because we all care about the students."

"Wow, that's so powerful," I say, pausing to reflect on what she just said. I continue. "Those are all the questions I have for you. Is there anything else you want to share with me?" "Yeah," she starts, "I identify as a Mexican American. I identify with the Latino community, and that's essential. I am just like the students. I came from where they come from. I am from their neighborhood. At the same time, my formal education has always been in English. To me, that's a dominant part of my personality. Despite that difference, I feel very connected to the students. I feel at home in a Spanish-speaking institution where I'm able to continue learning and perfecting my Spanish too. I feel welcomed here. I transfer that connection to the students, and that is important. We grow together."

I thank her again as I wrap up the interview. "Thank you, *Profesora*, for your time. This has been very informative. I am going to finalize my story this afternoon, and I will share it with you once it is finished." She enthusiastically agrees. "Yes, please, I want to see it when you are done. Thank you for taking the time to get to know more about us and for sharing our story with others. We sort of fly under the radar, but we like it like that. We don't want people to bother us. Just leave us alone and let us do what we do." We both laugh. "Absolutely," I agree, "And you do it well!" I get up and reach out to bid her farewell. We hug each other and kiss one another on the cheek. She wishes me good luck, "*Suerte. Take care.*"

Theorizing Latinx-serving as an Organizational Third Space

Friday night. 11:00 pm. I submit the article to my editor. I am satisfied with what I wrote, but I am not done investigating APC. I continue to reflect on my experience as an undergraduate student at a predominantly white, highly selective institution in the city. I remember the time that a white student asked me about my experience in the special admissions program on campus, assuming that I was a special admit—admitted despite the fact that my GPA and test scores were just below the minimum necessary for regular admission, but high enough to show my potential. I remember what it felt like to be presumed incompetent because of the color of my skin or my last name. If I had known then what I know now, I would have asked him what it was like to be admitted through the legacy program, because clearly he was only admitted because his dad donated a lot of money to the institution. But I wasn't ready with the comeback; the sting was too sharp, and the salt in the wound was too painful. It was a pain I hadn't experienced until college, when I was immersed in a white world for the first time—a world that sees me as unmotivated, uneducated, undocumented, and unworthy of admission to one of the best (and whitest) institutions in the country.

I wonder if I would have attended APC if I had known about it when I was in high school. Probably not. I had been convinced, like everyone else in the United States, that white is good, and because highly selective institutions are mostly white, they're usually good. But the one I attended was not good for my soul, for my cultural self, or for my commitment to working with and for my community. I wasn't taught those things in college. I feel somewhat jealous of the students who attend APC. What a remarkable opportunity it is to attend an institution that presumes you are competent and worthy, and that thinks your language and culture are beautiful assets to be enhanced, not subtracted. I remember a recent theory I read about called third space, which is a place where discordant discourses come together to create a transformative learning environment. As Gutiérrez (2008) argues, however, these spaces, "should not be considered a utopian narrative, as work in these spaces is difficult and filled with contractions, setbacks, and struggle" (p. 160). APC must not be taken for granted, as the administrators, faculty, and staff there are actively working to transform the space into one that is discursive yet relevant, personal, and transformative.

I flip back through the journal articles I read to prepare for the interviews and write this story. While the third space has been described at the classroom level (Fitts, 2009; Gutiérrez et al., 1995; Hadi-Tabassum, 2006; Moje et al., 2004), I did not come across any articles that describe it at an institutional level, perhaps because these types of institutions are nearly nonexistent in the United States. Moje and colleagues (2004) propose that there are at least three conceptualizations of third space, including one that views this space as a bridge between dominant and minoritized perspectives; a second that views it as a navigational space, where multiple discourses are explored within a nonbinary setting; and a third that merges cultural, social, and epistemological knowledges as a way to challenge dominant ways of knowing while enhancing learning. In thinking about each of these, I draw three boxes, imagining a third space at the institutional level.

At the population level, I consider all the measures used to determine the effectiveness of a postsecondary institution. How do we know whether an institution is adequately serving (Latino) students? Legislators want institutions of higher education to be accountable, affordable, and "high quality" (Espinosa et al., 2014), with some states implementing outcomes-based funding models that require institutions to show measurable input, progress, process, and output metrics (Jones et al., 2017). It is also expected that institutions will graduate students in a reasonable amount of time (arbitrarily defined as six years). Moreover, the dominant white measures that have historically been used to evaluate

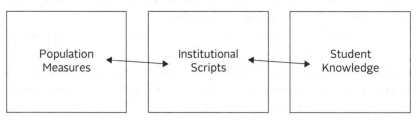

Figure 4. Preliminary Model of an Organizational Third Space.

and assess institutional effectiveness include selectivity, research dollars, and the subjectively measured "talent" of faculty and students (Astin, 2016). As noted by the administrator I interviewed, APC strives to meet the dominant white ideals set by those external to the organization by providing a low-cost, high-quality education that adheres to the standards of the Higher Learning Commission. These are the dominant population measures that legitimize all postsecondary institutions (Garcia, 2017). Yet conformity is limited at APC, as it is not a prestigious research university, and it is not concerned with meeting white measures of institutional effectiveness and prestige. This is where it diverges from the population scripts as constructed by the dominant culture.

The students bring with them their own cultural ways of knowing as well as a variety of linguistic abilities that the institution legitimizes and validates. The institution not only recognizes the minoritized, racialized epistemologies of its students; it actively seeks them out through recruitment and engagement with the Latino community, in person and through Spanish-language media. The faculty and staff contribute to this ethos by offering their language and cultural epistemologies to the institution. A large percentage of the faculty and staff identify as Latino and many as Spanish speakers, including those in offices that provide support to students, such as financial aid. These social identities are reflected in the organizational identity, which stresses its bilingual identity as a core part of who the institutions is (Garcia, Ramirez, Patrón, & Cristobal, forthcoming). Even for faculty who do not share the same language and cultural backgrounds as the students, their scripts reinforce participation structures that are nonnormative, with faculty encouraging students to "say it in Spanish, we'll figure it out," which allows for the emergence of a multi-voiced social heteroglossia (Gutiérrez et al., 1995). This reinforces the minoritized identities of students, faculty, and staff, who then feel validated and confirmed in the space. The presence of actors with multiple ways of knowing and being transforms the institution, as they become the institution.

The institutional scripts conform to the expectations of the population, but only to the extent necessary. The dominant institutional scripts are unapologetically and historically committed to access, starting as a grassroots effort, with one site in the city. As the Latino population expanded outward, the institution expanded with it, adding additional sites in the city and on its outskirts. The founders of the institution saw a tre-

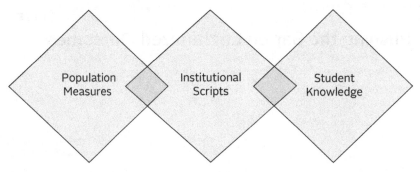

Figure 5. Model of an Organizational Third Space.

mendous need to serve a community that was being oppressed and discriminated against, including being misdiagnosed with mental illnesses. The founders had the sole intention of educating Latinos and helping them get a job. Moreover, the institution was founded in a city that has historically discriminated against Latino people at the educational, social, and political levels (Garcia & Hudson, 2019), creating a tremendous need for a nonnormative institution. The institution admits students who would not be admitted to other postsecondary institutions, which is an important endeavor. Some students have even dropped out of high school, but this is not considered a deterrent, as the institution offers a GED program. In fact, in doing my research, I learned that the GED program was one of the original programs offered.

Beyond access, the ethic of care and support is embedded within the institutional scripts. In the classroom, faculty are patient with English-language learners, recognizing that some students are becoming proficient in English while also learning the subject. This is a challenge that is noted and understood. Affordability is also in the institutional scripts. Organizational members construct the institutional identity as low cost and high aid, with a particular interest in graduating students with minimal debt. Finally, the institutional scripts see students as able to succeed through earning a degree, getting a job, and pursuing an advanced degree. Beyond these traditional measures of success, the institution expects students to go back into their communities and empower others to pursue opportunities that will lift the Latinx community. I look back at my three boxes, tilt them slightly, and overlap them to represent the emergence of a third space at the institutional level.

FIVE

Pushing the Bar on Legitimized Outcomes

COLLEGES AND UNIVERSITIES in the United States function within a highly institutionalized field, meaning they follow patterns of isomorphism; they tend to become more and more alike over time, and they are highly influenced by the economic, social, political, and historical environments (Birnbaum, 1983; DiMaggio & Powell, 1983; Morphew, 2009; Suddaby, 2014). Institutional theory suggests that in the aggregate, disparate organizations become more similar as the result of three powerful forces: normative pressures, mimetic processes, and coercive isomorphism (DiMaggio & Powell, 1983). Individual postsecondary organizations in the United States have largely been influenced by these forces, leading to "structuration," or "the process of institutional definition," and the establishment of the postsecondary field (DiMaggio & Powell, 1983, p. 148).

Normative pressures are those that stem from the professionalization of a field, including pressures set by professional networks and organizations (DiMaggio & Powell, 1983). For colleges and universities in the United States, normative pressures come from the numerous organizations that represent them, including the American Council on Education (ACE), the American Association of State Colleges and Universities (AASCU), the Association of Public and Land-grant Universities (APLU), and the National Association of Independent Colleges and Universities

(NAICU), each with its own influencing powers over the institutions that it represents as well as over the entire field of higher education. For racialized organizations, such as Hispanic-Serving Institutions, there are more specific associations that apply normative pressures on organizations.

The Hispanic Association of Colleges and Universities, for example, is recognized as the voice for HSIs in the United States, with its main role being to push for legislative action that benefits Latinx students and HSIs collectively. HACU is essential to shaping the postsecondary landscape for HSIs; however, it primarily influences the environment within which organizations function, rather than directly dictating what individual institutions should do. This may be why HSIs spend so much time thinking about and talking about what it means to actually serve Latinx students. Since associations like HACU don't actually dictate what HSIs should or must do in order to better serve Latinx students, HSIs often look to each other. This is where other isomorphic pressures come in, such as mimicry.

The *mimetic process* is typically evoked when there is uncertainty and ambiguity within organizations, with each looking to others for models (DiMaggio & Powell, 1983). With so much organizational diversity within the postsecondary environment, colleges and universities are likely to mimic similar types of institutions. For example, small private colleges are more likely to model themselves after other small private colleges. For HSIs, there are fewer models to mimic. HSIs operate in a highly uncertain environment with few guidelines for how to serve Latinx and other minoritized students.

As a result, HSIs typically turn to other HSIs for best practices. This is evident with the Alliance of Hispanic-Serving Institution Educators (AHSIE), whose core function as a professional association is to support HSI educators through networking, information sharing, collaboration, and partnerships (AHSIE, 2017). AHSIE is a source of mimicry, which is essential for those HSIs looking for models and best practices in an uncertain environment. Excelencia in Education's *Growing What Works* database also has an important mimetic function, as HSIs can turn to the database for examples of academic programs, support services, and special initiatives that are working for HSIs across the United States (Excelencia in Education, 2017b). The database includes a wealth of information for HSIs to draw on at the associate, baccalaureate, and graduate levels across two- and four-year institutions. Moreover, the Department of Education annually posts the abstracts of projects that are awarded Title V Developing HSIs program grants, which are available to HSIs looking to the field for models of what is working in serving Latinx students and what is being funded by the federal government to do so (US Department of Education, 2016).

The third force, *coercive isomorphism*, results from pressure placed on organizations by other organizations, particularly those with legal and governing powers (DiMaggio & Powell, 1983). In the postsecondary landscape, there are numerous sources of coercive pressure to which organizations respond, including state and federal higher education legislation, nonprofit organizations and foundations, community groups, and parents. Colleges and universities react to these forces, yet they also have the ability to simultaneously apply pressure on them through lobbying and advocacy work. With education policy falling under state jurisdiction, states typically are the most powerful of all coercive forces influencing postsecondary education. In particular, state governments "shape institutional behavior by providing information on state goals, institutional performance, and best practices, among other matters," often under the guise of state governing boards (Dougherty & Natow, 2015, p. 14).

Since the late 1970s, with the rise of the educational accountability movement, nearly one-third of all states have turned to some form of performance and outcomes–based funding (POBF) policies (Dougherty & Natow, 2015; Jones et al., 2017). State governments implemented legislation that would be used to determine budgets for state-funded colleges and universities, with an initial focus on input (enrollment), progress (credit accumulation and persistence), and process (efforts to increase outcomes) indicators, and an eventual shift toward outcome indictors (retention, graduation, and job placement) (Dougherty & Natow, 2015; Jones et al., 2017). Policy-based research suggests that for racialized institutions, such as Historically Black Colleges and Universities, that have the infrastructures in place to serve minoritized students, POBF may not penalize them, but these policies provide little incentive for transforming the actual structures that would affect outcome indicators for minoritized groups (Jones et al., 2017). Although POBF looks different in every state, with varying emphases on different indicators over time and with disparate effects for individual colleges and universities, it is an example of a coercive legitimizing force that has shaped the postsecondary landscape for both public and private institutions.

What Are Legitimized Outcomes for HSIs?

The debate still remains about what it means to effectively serve Latinx students. While HSIs have emerged as a distinct organizational form, they are still susceptible to the norms and pressures of the postsecondary field, especially as organizations intentionally and unintentionally align themselves with the values and priorities of the field. As such, HSIs continue to evaluate their effectiveness as "Hispanic-serving" based on white hegemonic standards set by the field through normative, mimetic, and coercive pressures, with little regard for the unique needs and experiences of Latinx students. There is also a failure to recognize the heterogeneity within the Latinx population, with an assumption that to be "Hispanic-serving" looks one way, when in reality, there are multiple ways that it could look and feel, depending on the diversity of the Latinx population within different institutions in different regions of the United States. When the question arises about what it means to actually serve Latinx students, common legitimized measures of institutional effectiveness are persistence and graduation rates, with research supporting the use of these types of outcomes data to determine effectiveness (e.g., Contreras et al., 2008; Flores & Park, 2015; Garcia, 2017; Rodríguez & Calderón Galdeano, 2015). Policies such as POBF further solidify the narrative that beyond enrollment, progress toward outcome-based measures and processes that enhance those outcomes are legitimate (Jones et al., 2017).

Beyond graduation rates, however, what might be used as measures of institutional effectiveness for HSIs? Arguably there are other important outcome indicators, such as enrollment in postbaccalaureate degree programs and job placement following college (Garcia, 2017). Looking to the field might also reveal other indicators of institutional effectiveness. In 2017, the top ten state-level policy issues, according to the AASCU, included funding amid declining state budgets, affordability, student debt management, economic and workforce development, institutional productivity and student success, dual enrollment, support for undocumented and DACA (Deferred Action for Childhood Arrivals) students, and social issues, such as sexual assault, guns on campus, civil rights, academic freedom, and campus activism (AASCU, 2017). Similarly, the American Council on Education's (2017) core advocacy areas include budget and appropriations, financial aid, tax policy, health care, immigration, labor and employment, and veteran legislation. The NAICU (2016) has centered its advocacy work on student aid, tax policy, and higher education regulation, while APLU (2017) has focused on federal budget and appropriations, higher education policy and student aid, research and science, agriculture and natural resources, technology transfer and intellectual property, internationalization, and tax and finance policy.

In 2017, HACU's main legislative priority was to ensure continued and increased funding for HSIs, since they receive an average of sixty-nine cents for every federal dollar granted to all postsecondary institutions (HACU, 2017). HACU knows well that HSIs cannot and will not effectively serve Latinx students until the federal government addresses these funding inequities. In addition to advocating for increased funding for HSIs through the Department of Education's Title V Developing Institutions program and the centering of HSIs within subsequent reauthorizations of the Higher Education Act, HACU also focuses on increasing P-20 partnerships and enhancing STEM education by pushing for increased funding through such federal agencies as the National Science Foundation and the Department of Agriculture (HACU, 2017).[1] What these institutionalizing pressures suggest is that other outcomes may be good indicators of the extent to which HSIs are serving Latinx students, including college affordability, low student debt ratios, financial aid, economic and workforce development, and contributions to STEM fields.

Producing Outcomes at Rosado Private University

This counterstory is about Rosado Private University, the newest HSI among those in the study (i.e., the most recent of the three to meet the 25% enrollment threshold). From a field-level perspective, RPU is meeting many of the high-performance indicators of an effective institution, including graduating students at above-average rates compared to similar institutions, graduating students at equitable rates for all racial/ethnic groups, cutting time to degree, minimizing student debt, and training students to immediately enter lucrative careers upon graduation. This composite story uses data from one-on-one interviews with faculty and staff, focus groups with students, ethnographic observations at the main campus, website reviews, and document analysis of reports produced by the institution. I drew on the data collected, the theoretical foundation provided by institutional theory, and my own personal and professional experiences as a higher education professional and scholar (Solórzano & Yosso, 2002).

In developing this counterstory, I theorize a *Latinx-producing* organizational identity (Garcia, 2017). HSIs looking for a model to mimic could learn a lot from RPU. Based on field-level measures, RPU is effective and likely to be called a "good" HSI by researchers, legislators, and practitioners; that is, it is producing legitimized outcomes. Yet RPU also operates from a Latinx-neutral perspective, meaning it enrolls the minimum percentage of Latinx students to be eligible for the HSI designation while offering few opportunities for Latinx students to experience, enhance, or sustain their racialized and cultural ways of knowing (Garcia, 2018b). The narrator of this counterstory is Amy, a mixed-race transfer student at RPU who, for a class project, is creating a video documentary about RPU. Amy likes RPU, but he is critical of the institution's general exclusion of racially minoritized people, especially because he transferred from an institution that provided spaces and opportunities for racially minoritized people to engage with others like themselves, along multiple lines, including language and culture. Amy is in the process of interviewing people for his video project.

The Documentary

8:35 am. I step off the L, walk up the stairs, and immediately feel the cold breeze of this early November day in Chicago. I zip up my jacket and cross my arms, wishing I was anywhere but this cold city, perhaps Miami or Los Angeles. I walk quickly to RPU, which is only two short blocks from my CTA (Chicago Transit Authority) train exit. I notice a new exhibit in the window of the art museum on the ground floor of the building that is home to RPU, but I don't bother to look because I want to get out of the cold and into the building as quickly as possible. I enter the building through a revolving side door and immediately feel warmer.

I walk down the main hall and then turn the corner to catch an elevator to the third floor. I greet the guard and quickly flash my student ID. "Hey, Michael," I say, stopping at the guard podium. "Please tell me why it is so cold in November?" Michael laughs and tells me to stop being a cry baby. "It's Chicago, what do you expect?" I roll my eyes and keep walking, sticking my foot into the elevator door before it closes, much to the chagrin of the people in the elevator. I step in and say, "Good morning, everyone." Silence. I face the doors and roll my eyes again as I press the number "3."

When the elevator doors open, I step off and walk down the hall, before turning left and heading to the main corridor on the third floor. I walk into the Advising Center and greet the student employee at the front desk, reaching across the counter to hug her. "Hey boo, what's good?" She responds, "Just waiting for my shift to end at noon." I look at my watch and say, "B, it's 9:00 am, your shift just started!" She retorts, "And? You don't know my life. I have things to do." I laugh and say, "Girl, please! Is Lisa around?" She gestures with her right hand, indicating that Lisa is in her office. I thank her and walk back, stating, "Don't worry, I'll see you in a few, 'cause you'll still be working when I am done talking to Lisa."

I walk up to Lisa's office and see her talking to a student. Lisa, a white woman, is my academic advisor. I pop my head in and wave, but I don't say anything. Lisa smiles and says, "I'll be done in two minutes." I respond, "Take your time." Meanwhile, I fumble with the video camera that I checked out from the art department. It's nothing fancy and probably not much better than my iPhone camera, but I feel professional using it to make my video—like a real documentarian. I hear Lisa assuring the student that the class she has enrolled them in will count toward the degree requirements, ensuring a summer graduation.[2] The student is excited, realizing that they have finished their bachelor's degree in just three short years. Lisa finishes, "Call or text me if anything comes up, or if you need anything else or have any more questions." The student walks out smiling, and I walk into the office. "Are you ready?" Lisa replies even as she continues typing on the computer, "Yes, give me one second." I set up the video recorder facing Lisa. She looks up and laughs, "Oh, I didn't know the camera was going to be that close to my face." I quickly respond, "Yes, all up in your face, so that I know if you are telling the truth." We both laugh. Lisa finishes typing, looks up, and says, "I'm ready!"

I begin talking about the video project. "As I mentioned when I asked you to participate in this project, I am making a video about RPU, highlighting the aspects that make RPU a good institution when it comes to graduating successful students. It's in the form of a documentary, so it's based in truth and reality, told from the perspective of real people. I thought you would be a great person to interview, because as an academic advisor, you interact with many students and know a lot about the school's policies, procedures, and history." I pause, and Lisa chimes in, "Yes, I am happy to participate. I love RPU. It's such a wonderful place to work and a great place for students." I continue, "Let's get started. I am going to ask you a series of questions. Feel free to start and stop as needed, as I am going to edit the video anyway. If you mess up or want to change your answer, just start over. Make sense?" Lisa smiles, "Yes!"

I fumble with the video recorder again, looking into the camera, "Test, test." I turn the camera back around and see the red light to indicate that it is recording. "OK, it's on. To begin with, just tell me your name—first name only is fine—your position, and how long you have been here at RPU." Lisa begins, "I'm Lisa. I am an academic advisor. And I have been at RPU for seventeen years, first as a student for three and a half years, and now as an employee for thirteen years. I also got a master's degree in business management while I was working here. So, I have two degrees from RPU, and a lot of experience here."

I then prompt her, "Tell me what you like about RPU." Lisa looks down, looks back up at the camera, and shakes her head. "I think this is a wonderful place. I have been here seventeen years because it is just wonderful." I jump in, "What makes it wonderful?"

Lisa's face lights up. "To begin with, students are successful at RPU. They come here, and they graduate, and they get jobs. Also, they can earn their degree in three years if they take three classes each term, including the summer, because it's an accelerated program, so they have the option to work quickly if they want to. Of course, some students can't do that, because they are working full-time and have families, but we offer them flexibility so they can take two classes at a time. That way, they can finish fast, and that is powerful. The last I heard, 97% of our graduates complete within four years, which is unheard of, but it's because we have five quarters per academic year. We push them to finish fast and not linger too much, because they're losing income in a way, right? We want them to graduate and start their careers, and we do whatever we have to in order to help them do that." I interrupt, "How do y'all do that? If other colleges wanted to graduate students in four years or less who also get jobs, what should they do?"

Lisa continues, "We are very intentional in what we do, and all the faculty and staff believe in what we do. We provide students the opportunity to get a degree quickly, and we offer career training along the way. But I would say that it starts with recruitment and admissions. An admissions counselor works with students on admissions *and* financial aid, rather than having them go from the admissions office to financial aid. That way they continue working with one person they are already comfortable with. Financial aid is usually more unfamiliar to students in the early stages of the enrollment process. We coach them through the process. We offer them financial support based on their academic abilities and their talents, including their athletic talents. We offer scholarships; some are based on ACT scores, while others are based on a student's desire to play sports while at RPU. When a student is admitted, if they have a social security number, they have to fill out a FAFSA (Free Application for Federal Student Aid) and apply for MAP and a Pell Grant. That allows us to get that money from the state to help cover the student's tuition. Every student gets a different amount based on their income and all of that. We are meeting their needs so that no one pays more than $7,500 out of pocket per academic year at this campus. We are committed to graduating students with a low debt rate, and we are delivering on that. Our students don't graduate with very high debt."

I add, "That scholarship is the main reason I came to RPU. How could I pass up a full scholarship to a private institution? I ain't no fool!" We both laugh. I continue, "One thing you said is that *if* students have a social security number they apply for MAP and Pell. What about those who do not have one?" "Good question," Lisa begins. "I am not a financial aid advisor, so you might want to interview someone in that area, but from what I understand, for undocumented students, there are ways to give them scholarships. Undocumented students can't apply for MAP and Pell Grants. If they don't get those, then we cover what they would have gotten had they had a social security number and been able to apply for FAFSA. I think that's really cool, because we're giving them the money that they would have been able to get from the state and federal government. I am not sure how it works, but someone in financial aid can probably tell you the details. I have not advised very many undocumented students here at the main campus, but when I was working at the branch campus about forty-five minutes outside of the city, I had more, as that campus is about 80% Hispanic, and some of those students were undocumented. That's when I learned about what it means to be undocumented, because I had never thought about that before."

I look back at my note pad. "Scholarships are important here at RPU. What else does RPU do to help students graduate in less than four years and get jobs?" Lisa lights up again, "Advising, of course—that's what I do. Starting at the very beginning of the enrollment process, we're meeting with students one-on-one, rather than everything just taking place online. We're much more active with the process with the students to help them identify what it is they want to do. We focus more on one-on-one interactions because we know that many students that we serve have a lot of questions and have some fear, and they don't necessarily have a support network or an understanding of how college works. Their parents may not have gone to college. That's a huge challenge, not just for the students but also for their families, because they don't necessarily have the background or understanding to help students in the college process. I think providing support through advising is so important. Sometimes it's just being there to let them come in and vent, or to sort through their thoughts about how they're going to talk with their parents about how they can't go to Mexico for the next three weeks because they have to be in class. We help them to solve problems, and we're an ear for them. We listen, and eventually they figure it out. They sometimes need someone to just listen. So, I listen. That's my job.

"We've also asked faculty to step up and serve more in an advisory role. In a lot of situations, especially with first-year students, I think that's helped, because we as advisors are not in the classroom with them. We don't see them on a regular basis. When you have a faculty member who can recognize when someone walks in the door, whether they're gloomy that day or something is going on with them, then the faculty member can check in more easily with the student. Having multiple advisors—and multiple people to care for students—is important.

"We also have a cohort model of education here, so the students don't pick their classes; they are assigned to courses by their advisors. That is essential to them matriculating and graduating on time. We have a very aggressive, intensive academic advising approach, and that is why students graduate. Overall, I think we create this environment where students get a lot of support through their faculty, through their advisors, through their coaches, if they are student athletes. I think that is the key to it all."

I smile. "I feel like if I didn't already go to school here, I would want to, because that was so moving and motivational!" Laughter erupts. I ask a clarifying question, "Do you have any special advising or programs for racial or ethnic groups? At my old school, we had a program for minority students, and we had special advising and services through that program." Lisa pauses for a moment. "We have a Title III grant, and I think they do some special advising, but for the most part, we've always treated every student the same. We've always had a very aggressive, intensive academic-advising approach. That approach was there regardless of whether the student was Hispanic, African American, white, whatever. I think, sometimes, when we see difference—when we treat people differently—it's because they are more academically at risk. That's when, maybe, we'd have an additional intervention. Otherwise, I think that services and advising are focused across the board for all students. I don't think we look at race, but at academic need for all students to be successful."

I nod. "Thanks for clarifying. Financial aid and advising are important for graduating students on time and with low debt, regardless of race or ethnicity. Can you talk about the career preparation aspect? How do you prepare students for careers and ensure that they get jobs?" Lisa replies, "We focus on incorporating career development and training into the curriculum, and we require students to have an internship as well. We believe that if you have the experience and you have the training, then you're able to get a job at graduation. All of our students have an internship before they graduate. The majority of our students actually complete two or three internships. When you look at the types of companies that we work with, we have a wide mix of businesses, including minority-owned and Fortune 500 companies, community organizations, social service organizations, and healthcare providers. I think that by having a wide variety of experiences with different types of companies and organizations and in different types of neighborhoods, students get exposure to the skills they need to get a job.

"We also incorporate career management training into the curriculum. Each academic year, students have to take a career management training course. They take a total of four of these courses before they graduate. Within those courses, they develop their resumes, practice interviewing, and make connections with potential employers. It's very intentional. We also offer experiential learning in a majority of our courses and degree programs. Those classes that are experiential take students out of the classroom and into the city, to a museum or to local neighborhoods; then the students reflect on what they learned in the city and how they can apply those skills in other areas of their studies. Our focus has been on experiential learning for a long time. Back in the day, a lot of people didn't think that was a legit thing. Now, you hear people talking about experiential learning and experience-based education all the time, and it's something that we've always done. When students learn by doing—through internships, assimilations, and practicums—they get the skills that they need to be successful. When they leave here, they don't need to be trained in how to do something because they've already done it."

I nod in agreement. "I'm going to stop you right there. You have provided me with so much great footage already, and I have to get to class." Lisa laughs and says, "That was fun." I stop the recorder as Lisa continues. "This really is a good place, you know? We care about students, and we want all students to be successful. We believe in students, and we believe in ourselves." I put the video recorder back into my bag and bid farewell to Lisa. "I'll holler at you later. I have to ask you a few questions about next term. But first let me get to class so that I don't fail this term." Lisa waves and turns back to her computer.

* * *

2:36 pm. I wait in the library for my friend Anabel who has agreed to participate in the documentary. The librarian has allowed me to set up the video camera in a corner near the large windows that overlook that city. The setting is perfect for a video, as I can capture both a view of the city and a row of contemporary bookshelves that line the library. This is no ordinary library; the bookshelves look like they came straight out of IKEA. Some are tall, and some are waist high. It has a special feel. I look at my watch, then look up to see Anabel approaching. She waves as she approaches the table. "Sorry I'm late, I was talking to my advisor in the hall." "Whatever, girl," I reply. "I'm done for the day. What about you?" Anabel responds, "I'm going home after this, although I don't want to go out there. It looks freezing!" I nod my head in agreement. "Don't get me started."

"Go ahead and sit here so that I can get a good backdrop for the video," I direct her. I have already set up the video camera, and I am ready. "Let's get started. I already told you that this interview is for a class project. I am making a documentary about RPU, highlighting what makes it a unique place. Feel free to start and stop as needed, or if you need to, start over, because I will edit the video. Just be honest. This documentary is about the real-life experience of people at RPU." Anabel nods in agreement. I prompt her, "To start, state your first name, your major, and your year in school." "I'm Anabel, I am a nursing major, and I am a junior," she says. I continue, "I have interviewed several people already, and there seem to be some common themes about what makes RPU a good college, including financial aid, advising, career development, and experiential learning. Can you first talk about your experience at RPU with financial aid? Do you have a scholarship? How have you funded your education here?"

Anabel begins. "In high school, I was in this program called AVID (Advancement Via Individual Determination), which helped students with applying to college and working through that process. My counselor talked about a scholarship that RPU was offering for two students in my high school district, and I applied. I was one of the two students who got the scholarship. I'd never thought of coming to a university because my only two options were getting the scholarship or going to community college, because of my background. Being here and having the privilege of having that scholarship means a lot. Not a lot of people have that type of cash." I interject, "So you wouldn't have been able to come here if you didn't get the scholarship?" "Exactly," says Anabel. "But I am glad I did, because I feel like RPU does help you a lot, and then they also keep you on top of your scholarship if you have one. For example, for the scholarship that I got, you have to maintain a certain GPA. You can't slack off, because they're going know when you slack off, and they're going bring it to your attention. That's when you have to talk to them about what's going on. I feel like they motivate you as well, because you want to keep that scholarship."

I ask, "Anything else about financial aid and your experience that you want to share?" Anabel says, "I have one complaint about my financial aid advisor. He's always at lunch between 9:00 am and 3:00 pm. Every time I've gone in to see him, he's like, 'Come in tomorrow at this time.' I come in the next day, and I don't know if he tells the front desk people to say that he's at lunch or something, but he's never around. I end up canceling the appointment, but then I'll turn around, and he's walking out of his office. I'm like, 'I thought you were at lunch.' He'll say, 'I'm not at lunch. I'm going on lunch now.' I ended up telling him, 'Do you tell the ladies at the front to tell your students that you're at lunch? Because you seem to be at lunch from morning until evening.'" We crack up laughing.

Anabel continues. "Right now, I put up with it because I don't pay any tuition with the scholarship I have. My financial aid advisor has not always been available, and they've messed up on my paperwork multiple times. But I don't pay for school, so I can't complain. I know one of my classmates who is in the nursing program right now was paying tuition out of pocket. She was told that she didn't owe any money. Then three terms later she saw on her bill that she had a past due amount for $1,500. Then supposedly her tuition was past due, and they were going to put her in delinquent payments. She said that she didn't know about it until she got the notice. She never had a past-due balance before. She said she had paid cash up front for each of those terms, so they messed up. They said that they hadn't looked at her paperwork right and realized that they had been giving her too much money. They went back to those terms and took that money out. Then they put her in delinquent payment even though they made the error. That's happened to multiple people that I know. The financial aid office needs to get it together. A lot of us get scholarships and financial aid, so we just accept their poor customer service. But we shouldn't have to."

I agree, "That's right! Playing with my money is like playing with my emotions!" Laughter erupts. I continue, "You like the scholarship, but you don't like the service. What about your general academic advising experience? What has that been like for you?" Anabel tells me, "So far, my experience with my advisor has been pretty good. She has an open-door policy. Whenever I want to change my classes, I'll talk to my advisor, and she helps me with that. Or she'll help me get on a faster track to get out of here; she'll tell me where I'm at right now and what I need to do. She's very helpful. She asks questions just like an instructor would ask. We talk, and we just go from there. She talks with me about each of my classes. She says, 'Tell me how you feel about this class, how you feel about that class. Do you like your classes?' She asks me, 'Are you having any problems with your classes? Just let me know.' She's very caring. I like her.

"I can text her, even on the weekend, and if she needs to be on her computer to help me, and she's not home or she's not in her office, then she will tell me, 'Come to my office at this time and we'll discuss it.' She's knowledgeable about a lot of the scholarships that are given out. I know a lot of students prefer to go to their academic advisor even for financial issues, because many people have struggled with the financial aid office. I like my advisor, but I've heard bad stuff from other students, like 'My advisor sucks' or 'She hasn't gotten my stuff in.' Half the time, it's not even the advisor's fault. It's someone else in a different department's fault, but I also hear stuff that's bad about some advisors. I've never had that experience."

When Anabel pauses, I ask, "Anything else?" She continues, "No, I think that is it. I generally think the advisors are good and accessible and knowledgeable. They make the experience at RPU really good." I ask my next question. "What have your experiences been with career development and experiential learning?" Anabel jumps right in with excitement. "It's been wonderful. For nursing, we do clinicals at one of the biggest hospitals in the city of Chicago, as well as some smaller ones. RPU makes the experience good, and if you've done two clinicals at the same hospital, they try to put you at another hospital for your other required ones. They don't put us all at one hospital for the entire time. They make sure that we see different hospitals, because you're not going have the same patients at the different hospitals. They try to make sure that we see a diverse population."

I follow up, "Does RPU provide similar internship opportunities for all majors or just for nursing?" Anabel replies, "With nursing and all of the healthcare degree programs, we have a lot of clinical hours that we have to do. I have a friend who is in culinary arts, and they also do internships. One of my friends talked about doing a 'stage,' in which he got to shadow a chef for three or four hours a day. In our classes, we always talk about real-world applications, and we talk about getting a job when we're done. I think that is the case for all majors. I have heard the term *industry-based curriculum*, which I guess is a curriculum about your industry and how to succeed in that. They give us the tools to succeed in our industry."

I jump back in, "What about experiential learning? What has been your experience with that?" Anabel pauses for a moment. "I haven't had as much experience with that. In my art class, we went to the art museum. We get to go for free any time. We just show them our ID. Usually you'd have to pay $20, to go in there. The museum is huge. It's interesting. It's a cool place. A lot of professors take their classes there. You go to a certain section of the art museum and look at that form of art or at different cultures, and you take a picture. Then, in the next class period, we present about what we saw. I have also heard of professors taking students to Chinatown. Some classes take students out to do Junior Achievement, which is a program where you can work with youth in the community. For nursing students, we primarily stick to nursing clinicals and working in the hospitals. We don't have a lot of time for other things. I guess experiential learning is major specific." Anabel gets quiet, waiting for me to ask another question.

I begin, "One thing I have noticed, since I transferred here from another institution, is that there are not a lot of activities or programs for different racial/ethnic groups. At my old school, there was a multicultural center, and there were Africana Studies courses. You're Latina, right?" Anabel says, "Yes, Mexican American. I was born here, but my parents were born in Mexico." I continue, "What are your thoughts on that?" Anabel pauses for a moment as she thinks about the question. Then she speaks. "I speak English and Spanish. My parents mostly only speak Spanish, so I grew up speaking Spanish. But when it comes to medical terminology, I obviously don't know the terms in Spanish. It's a whole different language. Just because you speak Spanish doesn't mean that you know the medical terminology. It's very different when you're translating words. RPU started offering a class in which they teach Spanish medical terminology, especially for health studies. I think the class is new; they've only offered it one time. But we need it, so that's good. Other than that, I don't think there is anything for Mexican American students.

"My friend goes to another university in the city, and there is a group that you could join for Latino students, or everybody who is Hispanic could join. They have events like Cinco de Mayo. They also have nights where they have Mexican food, and everyone gets together. But here at

RPU, you don't see any events to celebrate heritage. I think there was a Chinese New Year celebration last year. I think sometimes they serve ethnic foods, but otherwise, there are not a lot of cultural events."

I interrupt Anabel and ask, "How do you feel about that?" Anabel states, "I understand why they don't have clubs like that. This is a small school compared to other schools. Maybe we do not need a Latino group, but I think it would be helpful to have events once in a while to add culture to the school. They don't have to create a group if there's not a lot of people who would join it. I would say it would be helpful to have days or events. I might feel more comfortable if they had more Mexican or Latino events. But maybe that is just me." I add, "I don't think it's just you. I want more cultural events and resources too. I'm mixed race and I speak French, and I don't feel like there is anything to help enhance those aspects of my identity at this school." Anabel jumps in and says, "I think it is important. I think culture should be more encouraged here in the institution because your goal before graduating is to become a well-rounded person. How do you become that if you don't talk about different races and cultures in class? Where do you learn it from?" I nod my head in agreement, "Exactly!" Anabel continues, "I think most classes are diverse. But I think it's important to elaborate on culture more. I think you learn by actually interacting with different kinds of people. Sometimes not everyone in your class will have the same opinion as you. There should be more activities in class that encourage us to meet each other and learn about each other."

Anabel stops to reflect more. "My friend also takes Latino Studies courses at her school. She loves it. She learns a lot about Latinos in the United States, such as all the protests and marches that Latinos have participated in here in Chicago and in Los Angeles and New York. I have never heard of a class like that here. I know a lot of people take a class about the Holocaust. I think it's a history and social sciences class about Germany and the Holocaust. I have never been able to take it, because we only get a few options for courses each semester. But I have heard it's pretty good, and it opens your eyes to the world. There are not a lot of options for taking courses about my own culture, besides that Spanish medical terminology class, which I am excited to take." I interject, "I want to take Africana Studies but there aren't any classes here. I took a few classes on Black history at my other institution before transferring here, and it was pretty cool. Anabel continues, "Also,

I have never had a Hispanic professor. The nursing faculty are knowledgeable, and they teach me what I need to know about nursing, but it's weird that the there are no Hispanic teachers here, at least not that I know of. In other classes that I have taken, I have seen some diversity, and I think it influenced the class. I wouldn't say it plays a big role, but I feel the teaching style is different, and that's what I feel helps you learn more."

I shake my head furiously, "I agree. Completely." I continue, "Those are all of the questions I have for you. I am going to turn off the video recorder now." I turn the camera off and thank Anabel for her insightful answers. "Thanks again for helping me out with this project." "No problem," Anabel responds as she stands up, looking out the window for a few moments before putting on her coat, because she knows it's going to be freezing out there.

Hypothesizing Latinx-producing: Color Neutral Legitimization

9:56 pm. I am back at home, going through the videos in search of the best clips for the documentary. The assignment is due tomorrow, so it's going to be a long night. I take a sip of pop and create a file on my computer called "Color Neutral Success." I think about the things I learned from the people I interviewed. None of them were a surprise to me, as I already knew what RPU did to help students be successful. I love my advisor, Lisa. She is always available and has helped me a lot, especially when I was transferring credits from my previous college, even though a lot of them didn't transfer over. I'm still annoyed about that. I also received a full scholarship, which is why I chose RPU when I transferred. I have friends at other colleges who have already taken out loans and are still struggling to pay their tuition each term. I understand how important it is for colleges to provide adequate financial aid. Since I started two terms ago, I haven't had any experiential-learning classes or internships, so that was useful to learn about. What I can't get over is that the people I interviewed did not talk about courses or programs for minoritized people. With so much diversity at RPU, I'm surprised by the lack of recognition of people of color.

The college I came from had a diversity center on campus. It had diverse teachers who spoke different languages, which was helpful for students like me who speak different languages. For me, it's French. I think in French. I listen to music in French. When it comes to certain things, the language doesn't always translate easily. I remember the time when I had to talk about myself in class, so that people could get to know me. In my introduction, there were some terms that didn't translate into English, so I had to explain to the class, "This means that." At my previous college, I could visit the diversity center and get help. If I wrote a paper, I could go to the diversity center and get help translating from French to English. RPU needs something like that for students.

RPU has high graduation rates and high rates of students who graduate in less than four years and get jobs. But at what cost to them? Is the structured education that RPU provides stripping minoritized students of their prior strengths and culture and teaching them to accept positions of powerlessness within society (Shor, 1992)? I'm struggling. I remember the sociology class I took my first year in college. I took it with an Afro-Latina professor who had the class read a book by Eduardo Bonilla-Silva titled *Racism without Racists: Color-blind Racism and the Persistence of Racial Inequality in America*. In the book, the author talks about four main ways that white people justify racism, or what the author calls "new racism," including "a network of social relations at social, political, economic, and ideological levels that shapes the life chances of the various races" (Bonilla-Silva, 2014, p. 26). I find the book on my shelf and flip through it, thinking about what Bonilla-Silva (2014) calls "color-blind racism." In reviewing the videos, I look for examples of the four frames.

Abstract liberalism is the use of ideologies associated with political and economic liberalism as a way to explain racial inequalities while sounding reasonable, moral, and ethical (Bonilla-Silva, 2014). This may manifest as rationalizing unfairness in the name of equal opportunity, utilizing meritocracy to argue that the most qualified people should gain the most advantage, arguing that the government should not intervene in social and economic matters, or suggesting that individual choice is the single most important determinant of success (Bonilla-Silva, 2014). Ronald, an Asian American student whom I interviewed, used this frame when I mentioned RPU's status as an HSI. Ronald asked me, "Why would one culture be treated differently? Why would that make senses? How come Chinese people don't get treated differently? It's not fair." I also consider Lisa's quote: "I must say I don't think we treat any of our students any differently. I've not been in a conversation where they said, 'We're going focus on this group of students and this is what we're going do specifically for them.' I think we treat them all the same. We want them all to have the same opportunities. Our ultimate goal is to get them graduated." What these quotes fail to recognize is that within the United States, equality does not translate to equitable outcomes. Treating people the same does not mean that everyone will get what they need to survive in an economically stratified system.

Naturalization is the use of language that suggests that racial inequities are a natural occurrence or that racial matters are the way they are naturally (Bonilla-Silva, 2014). In claiming naturalization, sociohistorical reasoning is diminished or ignored all together. One example is racial segregation in housing and education, which some argue is a natural phenomenon, without recognizing the sociohistorical policies and factors that have solidified a segregated society that also manifests inequities. I review a video clip from Jade, an African American woman, who talked about Junior Achievement, an experiential-learning program at RPU that allows students to work with low-income youth in the community. In her video, Jade expressed her concern that RPU sends students into communities economically affected by sociohistorical factors without specific knowledge of those communities. Jade said, "There was an Asian student on the bus. He was like, 'Oh, my goodness. We're going into the 'hood. I don't want to go into the 'hood. I'm going to end up getting shot.'" I wonder if RPU is fostering this naturalization framework within students by failing to talk about the specific factors that have led to racially segregated neighborhoods in Chicago.

The third fame, *cultural racism*, relies on culturally based arguments to explain racial inequities, which often include "blaming the victim" or suggesting that racially minoritized people lack the effort and values to succeed (Bonilla-Silva, 2014). I was surprised when Juanita, a Puerto Rican woman, stated, "People think every Hispanic drops out of high school because they either get pregnant or they just don't want to go above their careers to be that way. At my high school, since it was mostly white people, we all graduated. There wasn't anyone who didn't graduate or who dropped out. My cousin went to a Hispanic school, and she would say that people dropped out every single day because they were pregnant, they didn't want to finish school, or they weren't as motivated as some people." Juanita went on to say that she likes RPU because it enrolls a lot of Latinos. "People think that the norm is that Hispanic people drop out of school and have babies. But RPU shows people that not everyone is going do that. Everyone has their own future ahead of them. Sometimes you want to break the cycle and show people that you can be successful." I wonder if a curriculum that was more Latinx-centric would help disrupt students' internalized cultural racism while empowering them to challenge stereotypes in a more critical way.

The final frame, *minimization of racism*, relies on the argument that racism is no longer a problem, that people of color are hypersensitive when it comes to race, or that overt racism is the only unacceptable form of racism (Bonilla-Silva, 2014). When using this frame, whites may admit that discrimination exists but claim that it is not the cause of racial inequities, or they may find other nonracial reasons to justify inequities (Bonilla-Silva, 2014). I think about this frame for a while and realize that few people used this exact frame in their responses. One respondent, however, did say that at a private institution like RPU, students are discriminated against based on income, not race. This is a good point, and I wonder if students of color receive financial aid at the same levels as white people at RPU do. Operating from a race-neutral perspective, RPU is not likely to award financial aid based on societal differences in economic outcomes for people of color. I don't have any proof of this, but I contemplate it for a while.

* * *

11:02 pm. I am getting tired. I think I'll take a nap. I will finish the documentary when I wake up. Before closing my computer, I type the following notes to help me finalize the story I want to tell:

1. RPU graduates students in four years or less. (+)
2. RPU provides students with financial aid and scholarships. (+)
3. RPU provides career development and experiential learning. (+)
4. RPU has a good advising model. (+)
5. RPU is color neutral. (−)

Is operating from a color-neutral perspective a negative thing? What is the cost of success for students of color at an institution that does not recognize their racial and cultural ways of knowing? Are legitimized outcomes enough for racialized institutions like HSIs? Or should HSIs do more?

SIX

Reframing the HSI Narrative

IN THIS final chapter I offer suggestions for reframing the Hispanic-Serving Institution narrative around practice, research, and policy. Reframing the narrative means recognizing and highlighting the strengths and assets that HSIs offer the entire field of postsecondary education while acknowledging their unique position and challenges within the field as racially minoritized institutions. Reframing also means centering the voices and experiences of the people within these institutions, including students, faculty, staff, and administrators (Núñez, 2018).

First, I provide practical considerations for HSIs, highlighting what faculty, staff, and administrators working at HSIs and emerging HSIs can learn from the counterstories in chapters 3–5. Specifically, I offer information they can use in their daily practices as they strive to better serve Latinx and other minoritized students. I truly believe the practitioners working in HSIs are committed to improving their practices and policies for serving students, yet they struggle to find models and empirical research to draw from. One of the goals of this book has been to provide asset-based models and strengths-based research that practitioners can learn from.

I also provide my thoughts on the research and policy implications of the empirically grounded counterstories. I encourage scholars, legislators, and policy advocates to acknowledge the external forces that

HSIs are responding to on a daily basis, and I urge those developing future studies and policies to do the same. I remind readers that HSIs exist within a context that is grounded in whiteness and that they have been racialized as inferior within a racially white system. A second goal of this book, therefore, has been to disrupt the dominant white narrative of postsecondary research and policy, in hopes of finding more equitable ways of researching, evaluating, and advocating for HSIs.

Reframing Practice at HSIs

In chapters 3–5, I provided three counterstories based on empirical data collected over a two-year period in Chicago. The richness of the data, which were collected via a multiple-case study, was ideal for laying out thickly descriptive stories as told from the perspective of organizational members, including administrators, faculty, staff, and students. The stories provide information for constituents at HSIs and eHSIs to consider as they construct their *current* HSI organizational identity and, more importantly, as they think about their *ideal* HSI organizational identity (Garcia, 2017). In this section I refer to the counterstories to provide six practical considerations for better serving students in ways that may be counter to the dominant white narrative. I encourage institutions to consider these six suggestions as they reframe their practices for serving Latinx and other minoritized students. I caution readers that some examples may be more relevant to them than others, as they align more closely with other organizational characteristics (i.e., size, control, mission). This is important because I believe an HSI organizational identity is one of many identities that a college or university has. While the six considerations for practice are numbered, I do not believe that all HSIs can or should do all of these things.

1. **Provide curricula and programs that are grounded in justice and equity.** In chapter 3, I showed how organizational members at Azul City University actively construct an identity around providing an educational experience that is racially, ethnically, linguistically, and culturally enhancing by drawing on cues within the environment for enacting this type of identity. I introduced the idea that a Latinx-enhancing organizational identity is enacted through a social justice curriculum and culturally relevant programs, services, and practices. These types of curricula and programs should provide students with diverse perspectives,

teaching them about their own racial and cultural histories, but also about the history of other racialized, ethnic, and indigenous people. The curricula and programs should provide perspectives that are intersectional, including gender, sexual, religious, and socioeconomic identities. Moreover, they should be grounded in a liberation-based model, in which students learn about systemic subjugation and discrimination, with the goal of disrupting these systems. The curricula and programs should provide students with the tools to disrupt the injustices they may witness in their future workplaces and in their communities in general. This may also include civic engagement and activism. Within an organization where members construct this type of organizational identity, diverse curricular and programmatic offerings should be available and required for all, including people from dominant groups (e.g., white, male, heterosexual, high income, Christian).

2. **Hire faculty, staff, and administrators committed to justice and liberation.** In chapter 3, I also proposed that other indicators of a Latinx-enhancing organizational identity include hiring and retaining faculty, staff, and administrators who not only reflect the compositional diversity of the student population, but also are committed to justice for minoritized students and communities. Hiring faculty, staff, and administrators who look like the minoritized students in HSIs and who come from the same neighborhoods as students is essential, as national data suggest that the compositional diversity of the personnel at HSIs does not align with that of the student population (Garcia, 2018b; Gonzales, 2015; Santos & Acevedo-Gil, 2013). Yet these organizational members must also be committed to the liberation and justice of minoritized groups and have the training and background necessary to disrupt dominant ways of operating. Additionally, faculty, staff, and administrators from dominant groups must be on board with an agenda for justice and have the skills necessary for disrupting oppressive organizational structures. While organizational members at ACU did not feel that they were actively enacting this aspect of their organizational identity, they stressed its importance. Faculty, staff, and administrators at an institution that enhances the racial and cultural ways of knowing of minoritized students should be required to attend training and enhancement activities that challenge them to rethink diversity, inclusion, and justice for all. These activities should also raise their consciousness around the minoritization of multiple groups. Like the student-based curricula

and programs, faculty, staff, and administrators should learn from a liberation-based model, coming to understand that students enrolled in HSIs may struggle academically because of larger systemic issues. Faculty, staff, and administrators should be equipped to then make decisions and policies for students that are anti-deficit and asset based. Administrators must also support faculty and staff, recognizing their unique ways of knowing and empowering them to do the important work of enhancing the racial, cultural, ethnic, and linguistic ways of knowing of their students.

3. **Value and embrace nondominant input, process, and outcome variables.** In chapter 4, I theorized that an organization that enacts a Latinx-serving identity operates in a third space, as members at Amarillo Private College actively constructed their organizational identity in ways that extended beyond dominant scripts (Gutiérrez et al., 1995). Instead, organizational members constructed an identity that values access and success for Latinx and other minoritized students based on nondominant expectations. Members stressed the value of simply providing the Latinx community with options for postsecondary degree enrollment. They understood that APC is the *only* option for many of the students who enroll at APC, particularly because they provide access for students who may not have completed high school, may not speak English fluently, or may not have the income necessary to attend college. Simply being a broad-access institution, therefore, is important for a Latinx-serving institution. Organizational members at APC also stressed that while they want students to earn degrees and transfer to other institutions, they acknowledge that getting a GED may be the most important thing Latinx students can do for themselves and their families. Moreover, members emphasized that active engagement in the Latinx community is an important outcome for APC graduates.

4. **Reinforce bilingualism and the preservation of the Spanish language.** For institutions that construct a Latinx-serving identity, maintaining and enhancing the cultural and linguistic epistemologies of students is also essential, as reflected in the way that organizational members at APC constructed an identity that is grounded in bilingualism and culture. In chapter 4, I noted that by accepting and valuing the personal and sociocultural knowledge that students bring to higher education, APC is reflective of a third space, where dominant and minoritized discourses come together in order to create a new set of knowledge

and expectations (Gutiérrez et al., 1995). The centering of the Spanish language is essential to this third space and is unique to the institution. It's difficult to imagine any other postsecondary institution like this, as few postsecondary institutions operate as bilingual institutions. Yet other HSIs should learn from and emulate these practices as they seek to operate in a space where Latinx students succeed and develop in transformative ways. From APC, we learn that key aspects of a Latinx-serving identity include the preservation of the Spanish language and the reinforcement of bilingualism in an increasingly pluralistic society. At the same time, I want to stress that a majority of Latinx students who enroll in postsecondary education speak English fluently (Santiago, 2013), so bilingual education should be seen as an asset for Latinx students, not as a way to assimilate or acculturate them.

5. **Provide high-touch practices for students, including advising and experiential learning.** In chapter 5, I highlighted how Rosado Private University enacts a Latinx-producing identity through high-touch practices. Members at RPU stressed the importance of a strong advising model, with many of them calling their approach "intrusive advising." While this approach to advising is not innovative, it has been shown to increase the persistence and retention of low-income, first-generation students (Heisserer & Parette, 2002; Vander Schee, 2007), and it seems to be working for RPU; their persistence and graduation rates are comparable to non-HSIs (Garcia, 2018b). They require students to attend advising sessions every semester, and in those sessions, they tell students exactly which courses to take. This model leads to a quick time to degree, which is a desirable outcome in the field of postsecondary education. Other HSIs should certainly take note of the structured advising practices that RPU incorporates while recognizing that the size of the institution makes it possible to provide high-touch advising. A midsize or large institution would have to provide a significant amount of resources to their advising practices if they wanted to model the RPU advising model. Moreover, "intrusive" practices may not always be the best approach for students, as they may hinder the development of students as independent, empowered people. In fact, when I talked to students at RPU, they were concerned about their limited ability to choose electives.

A second way that members talked about the enactment of a Latinx-producing organizational identity was through the incorporation of experiential learning and internship opportunities that lead to post-graduation career attainment. Organizational members at RPU stressed the importance of students having access to at least two internship experiences over the course of their degree program. Moreover, they referred to Chicago as their backyard and an important source of experiential-learning activities. Again, other institutions must recognize that the location of the institution (Chicago) makes it possible to provide valuable internships and experiential-learning experiences to all students. Being situated in the heart of the city provides RPU with the ability to connect with large corporations, small nonprofits, and extensive healthcare networks, and allows access to the cultural, historical, and artistic resources in the city. This is not to say that an HSI located in a rural part of the United States cannot provide these types of experiences; they would just look different than they do for RPU. Working with migrant or indigenous populations in rural areas could certainly be considered important ways in which students could engage in experiential-learning opportunities while contributing to the development of those communities.

6. **Provide students with a diverse financial aid package.** In chapter 5, I also noted the importance of providing students with extensive financial support in order to retain and graduate them. In particular, organizational members at RPU stressed the use of scholarships and grants, rather than loans. This practice aligns with the general financial aid participation of Latinx students, as they are more likely to obtain grants and federal aid over loans (Santiago, 2013). I would be remiss if I didn't mention that privately controlled institutions such as RPU are better equipped to provide students with a well-balanced financial aid package, including covering full tuition for some students. RPU students also have access to the state-funded Monetary Award Program as well as the federal Pell Grant, which allows RPU to offer students a diverse package. In talking to students at RPU, however, many mentioned that they had in fact received "full-ride" scholarships. This is certainly a difficult practice to enact, and many HSIs, particularly those that are public and/or underfunded, will not be able to provide full funding to students. Yet the importance of providing a well-balanced financial aid package cannot be underestimated, as Latinx students, along with Black students, have the greatest need for financial aid and the lowest expected family contribution (Santiago, 2013).

Reframing HSI Research

This book, as well as my *Typology of HSI Organizational Identities* and the subsequent work from that theory (Garcia, 2017, 2018b; Garcia et al., forthcoming), are grounded in and seek to advance organizational theory; however, here I call on organizational theorists to recognize that most organizational theories are race neutral (Garcia, 2018a). I urge scholars to be more intentional in their use of race-conscious organizational theories and suggest a reframing of all HSI research in a way that recognizes the racial context within which HSIs are situated. In chapter 1 and in other publications, I have argued that HSIs are racially minoritized organizations that have been influenced, historically, by a racialization process and by the racialized identities of the people within them (Garcia, 2017; Garcia & Dwyer, 2018; Garcia & Hudson, 2019). This cannot be ignored as we conduct research with HSIs. In this section, I provide my thoughts on race-neutral organizational theory and its effects on the study of HSIs. I offer suggestions for future research while arguing that the most appropriate way to reframe the HSI research narrative is through race-conscious organizational theory (Garcia, 2015). While much of this section is grounded in the guiding theories of this book, recognizing that case studies are ideal for making analytic generalizations that extend current theory (Eisenhardt, 1989; Yin, 2009), I also draw on the counterstories in chapters 3–5 when appropriate.

Understanding HSIs through the Lens of Institutional Theory

The idea of HSIs evolved as a result of changes in the environment (i.e., demographic shifts in the population) and actions of leaders and advocates within the Latinx educational community (MacDonald et al., 2007; Santiago, 2006; Valdez, 2015). The federal recognition of HSIs in 1992 was an important victory for these leaders and advocates, as well as for Latinx college students and the postsecondary institutions enrolling the largest percentage of Latinx students. Recognition eventually lead to financial support in 1995, with federal appropriations to HSIs remaining steady over a twenty-year period (Santiago, Taylor, & Calderón Galdeano, 2016). While this recognition and support at the federal level suggests that HSIs are valued, they continue to fight for legitimacy. This battle is played out daily as practitioners, scholars, legislators, and policy advocates ask the perennial question, "What does it mean to be Hispanic-serving?" This question suggests that HSIs will not be seen as legitimate organizations until they can display and enact processes and practices that the field considers effective measures of serving Latinx students.

From an institutional perspective, legitimacy is the process whereby organizations seek recognition and validity from other organizations within the field. The process is shaped by a socially constructed reality about shared beliefs and understandings, and reinforced by regulation, legislation, and professionalization within the field (Scott, 1995). Legitimacy from this perspective is "not a commodity to be possessed or exchanged but a condition reflecting cultural alignment, normative support, and consonance with relevant rules or laws" (Scott, 1995, p. 45). Rather than adhering to rationality, organizations within a highly institutionalized field seek legitimacy by binding themselves to the myths and ceremonies that hold the field together (Meyer & Rowan, 1977). These rationalized myths are grounded in the meanings and understandings attached to the formal structures of the organization and the field, including policies, programs, functions, and rules (Meyer & Rowan, 1977). Organizations within a highly institutionalized field will only survive to the extent that they gain legitimacy through these processes (Scott, 1995).

Postsecondary institutions in the United States operate within a highly institutionalized field that is bound together by mimetic, normative, and coercive isomorphic pressures (DiMaggio & Powell, 1983). The field is shaped by other postsecondary institutions, legislation, and professional associations, all of which have different expectations of these educational organizations. Colleges and universities, therefore, are constantly responding to processes implemented by their aspirational peers, legislation at the state and federal level, and pressures applied by professional organizations that advocate with and for postsecondary institutions. In response to these pressures, postsecondary institutions seek legitimacy in a number of ways based on input, process, and outcome measures that have been determined to be desirable at a field level, including enrolling diverse populations, demonstrating progress toward degree for all students, and graduating students in a reasonable amount of time (Jones et al., 2017).

HSIs are susceptible to these same pressures, as there are few things that set them apart from racially white institutions. They are only unique in that they are compositionally diverse institutions, not only enrolling a large percentage of Latinx students, but also enrolling larger percentages of other students of color (i.e., Black and Asian American), low-income students, first-generation college students, immigrant students, and students whose first language is not English (Contreras et al., 2008; Núñez & Bowers, 2011). Beyond this compositional diversity, there are no distinct characteristics that set them apart from other colleges and universities, making it difficult to evaluate and assess HSIs as unique organizations. This is the essence of the debate about whether or not HSIs are actually "Latinx-serving" or simply white institutions that enroll a large percentage of Latinx students.

What this debate suggests is that HSIs not only should seek legitimacy in the same ways that other (white) postsecondary institutions do (determined by input, process, and outcomes variables), but also should *do more* than other (white) postsecondary institutions. This seems unfair considering that HSIs are typically under-resourced institutions with a limited ability to *do more* (de los Santos & Cuamea, 2010; Ortega, Nellum, Frye, Kamimura, & Vidal-Rodriguez, 2015). Moreover, federal appropriations to these institutions have hardly kept pace with the increasing number of HSIs, putting a great deal of pressure on HSIs to do more with less (Santiago et al., 2016). These tensions were most apparent in chapter 3, as organizational members at ACU grappled with what it meant to be an HSI, noting the importance of enrolling diverse students from Chicagoland and offering programs and services centered on the experiences of Latinxs, yet feeling defeated in recognizing that the racial composition of faculty and staff is behind that of the students, in hearing about the racism that people experience on campus, and in recognizing the systemic nature of the educational system in the city of Chicago that contributes to their inability to achieve the legitimized outcomes most recognized by the field.

I have argued that common measures of legitimacy for HSIs (i.e., institutional effectiveness) include reasonable/equitable six-year graduation rates (for Latinx students), postbaccalaureate degree enrollment (for Latinx students), and job placement (for Latinx students) (Garcia, 2017). These measures align with institutionalized ways of knowing in postsecondary education and are generally accepted as important outcomes for all colleges and universities. Yet, I also argue, based on research and grounded in cultural theory, that HSIs should provide positive campus climates (for Latinx students), support programs (for Latinx students), and community engagement (with the Latinx community) (i.e., *do more*) (Garcia, 2017). Chapter 4 provides a model for this type of environment, where students' cultural and linguistic knowledge are valued and celebrated in a caring, welcoming environment. These measures of effectiveness are not valued by political, social, and normative entities in the same way that institutionalized outcomes are, yet for over two decades, scholars have been arguing that they are essential to the retention and success of students of color in postsecondary institutions (e.g., Hurtado et al., 2012; Jayakumar & Museus, 2012; Rendon et al., 2000).

From the counterstories in chapters 3–5 and in other emerging work on the topic (e.g., Garcia et al., forthcoming), I have found that organizational culture may be a better theory for understanding what it means to be Latinx-serving. In chapter 3, I offered ACU as a model for a Latinx-enhancing organizational identity, as the most salient aspects of its HSI organizational identity are grounded in the cultural norms of working with and for the Latinx community in Chicago. In listening to members at APC make sense of what it means to be Latinx-serving, I found that they also drew on cultural cues about what it means to provide a caring and welcoming environment for Latinx students while providing curricular and programmatic experiences that are grounded in English–Spanish bilingualism. When asked what it means to be Latinx-serving, organizational members rarely talked about legitimized outcomes, instead focusing on the cultural elements that make them unique among the population of postsecondary institutions (Garcia et al., forthcoming).

This finding, that members construct identity based on cultural cues, disrupts and challenges the emphasis on the environment that is inherent in institutional theory, as HSIs may be better suited to drawing on cultural indicators of uniqueness. Because there are no ideal models for HSIs yet, meaning there are no colleges or universities that epitomize what it means to be Latinx-serving, it is difficult for HSIs to mimic other institutions. Instead, people within HSIs make sense of a Latinx-serving identity by looking at the elements that make them (seemingly) distinct from racially white institutions (organizational culture), rather than what makes them similar to other organizations (institutional theory), which Pedersen and Dobbin (2006) argue are two sides of the same theoretical coin. With the number of HSIs increasing every year, there must be more research that seeks to understand the multifaceted nature of an HSI organizational identity, drawing on Pedersen and Dobbin (2006) and extending my ideas about institutional and cultural theories. I encourage scholars to consider other organizational theories that will extend our knowledge of HSIs as organizations (see Garcia, 2015).

Legitimacy Considerations

While administrators, scholars, legislators, and policy advocates concerned with the education of Latinx college students should expect HSIs to seek field-level legitimacy while also transforming their structures into spaces that are welcoming, supportive, and culturally validating for Latinx students, there are a few considerations worth discussing. The first consideration is whether a significant change has occurred at the field level in order to allow for HSIs to evolve into unique legitimate forms. Arguably, HSIs have been striving for legitimacy based on the assumption that the postsecondary environment is stable. Yet Meyer, Brooks, and Goes (1990) remind us that environments are not always stable. Few scholars have theorized about the changing nature of the actual environment. Instead, theorists have spent extensive time and energy talking about change at the organizational level, and less time thinking about field-level change. Meyer et al. (1990) proposed that second-order changes (i.e., discontinuous change that leads to fundamental transformation) at the field level are revolutionary, as "industries are restructured and reconstituted during brief periods of quantum change, which punctuate long periods of stability" (p. 97). Change theorists propose that this type of change occurs as a result of a punctuated equilibrium, with equilibrium being a long-term state of stability, followed by "compact periods of qualitative, metamorphic change (revolution)" that "disassembles, reconfigures, and enforces wholesale transformation" (Gersick, 1991, p. 12). In order for punctured equilibrium to occur, the entire structure of a field must be dismantled to allow for a new configuration to evolve (Gersick, 1991).

Arguably there has not been a significant structural change at the field level that has led to the evolution of HSIs as a new organizational form. The most distinct thing about *federally eligible* HSIs is that they enroll a large percentage of Latinx undergraduate students. Yet some federally eligible HSIs do not even pursue the designation, let alone move into an identity construction phase. As such, the criticism is that beyond the 25% enrollment criteria, federally eligible HSIs continue to operate as other postsecondary institutions, legitimizing themselves based on standard (white) measures of institutional effectiveness (e.g., access, persistence/graduation rates, loan default). As long as HSIs continue to strive for these generally accepted, legitimized outcomes, the field will remain in equilibrium, with demographic changes representing only a small, incremental change, rather than a significant puncturing of the system. I have argued that in order for HSIs to fully liberate themselves, as well as their students and other organizational members, they must strive for outcomes beyond those legitimized by the field (Garcia, 2018a). This means embracing their role in democratizing education, developing critical consciousness, enacting civic engagement, encouraging involvement with minoritized communities, and working toward land preservation and environmental justice (Garcia, 2018a). This type of change may be necessary to punctuate the equilibrium that keeps HSIs striving for legitimacy based on white normative standards set by the field. Of the three institutions highlighted in this book, APC may be the best indicator of what a second-order change would look like in postsecondary education. In chapter 4, I called it a third space, yet through the lens of organizational change, the third space represents the point at which the equilibrium is punctured. With little research on the second-order change processes at the postsecondary field level, I encourage organizational theorists to consider exploring this topic more thoroughly with HSIs at the center of the analysis, turning to institutions like APC that operate outside of normative standards.

Racialized Legitimacy and Stratification

A second consideration is that within a society where white supremacy is the foundation, organizations strive for racialized legitimacy, without even recognizing or acknowledging it. Yet, institutional theorists have not accounted for the racialization process. Institutionalism and legitimacy have been theorized through a race-neutral lens, meaning that organizations are assumed to not have race. But as I argued in chapter 1, postsecondary institutions are racialized, historically, with white institutions considered legitimate, effective exemplars, and racially minoritized institutions (i.e., HSIs, HBCUs) considered lesser than and ineffective. In devaluing racially minoritized institutions, there is a failure to recognize that they are evaluated by white normative standards that have been legitimated by race-neutral research and policy. In this book, I argue that we can no longer conduct research with racially minoritized institutions through a race-neutral lens.

In failing to theorize about race and the process of racialization, organizational theorists have ignored the fact that race is an ongoing process within a society, like the United States, that is organized by race (Moya & Markus, 2010). As such, I argue that all organizations are affected by race, are assigned power and privilege based on race, and are evaluated based on physical and behavioral characteristics associated with race. Although Moya and Markus (2010) talk about racialization at the individual level, I draw on their ideas about "doing race" at an organizational level. Organizations, like people, do race based on historical social interactions, policies, and practices. Yet most research, policy, and legislative discussions about educational outcomes and inequities for racially minoritized students have remained at the individual student level, with little attention paid to the nature of the racialized organizations that enroll them.

While I have theorized an HSI organizational identity as socially constructed (Garcia, 2013a, 2016, 2017), in chapter 1, I made the leap to say that the racialized nature of the postsecondary educational system has led to the development of an HSI organizational identity that is racialized and considered inferior to racially white institutions. As suggested by Moya and Markus (2010), race is

> a complex system of ideas and practices regarding how some visible characteristics of human bodies, such as skin color, facial features, and hair texture relate to people's character, intellectual capacity, and patterns of behavior. According to this definition, race is a doing that involves several, often simultaneous, actions: (1) noticing particular physical characteristics like skin color, hair color, or eye or nose shape; (2) assuming that those characteristics tell us something general and important, such as how intelligent or how hard-working or conscientious a person is or has the capacity to be; (3) participating in the maintenance and creation of social and economic structures that preserve a hierarchy in which people associated with one race are assumed to be superior to people who are associated with another; and (4) justifying or rationalizing the resulting inequities. (p. 22–23)

This definition leads us to believe that race is connected to physical characteristics that tell us something about the character of the person possessing those characteristics; moreover, in recognizing race, consciously or subconsciously, we create and reinforce the social and economic structures that preserve a racial hierarchy that we then use to justify racial inequities. We do the same with organizations, recognizing that institutional characteristics differ and are often connected to the race of a college or university. For example, elite, well-resourced, research-intensive universities are often racially white, while racially minoritized institutions are more likely to be broad-access, less-selective, under-resourced comprehensive colleges (de los Santos & Cuamea, 2010; Ortega et al., 2015). These institutional characteristics are similar to the individual character, intellectual capacity, and patterns of behavior that Moya and Markus (2010) describe, and are used to subjugate those racially minoritized institutions that possess less-desirable characteristics within a system that is stratified by intelligence, resources, talent, selectivity, and prestige (Astin, 2016).

The racialization process that postsecondary institutions have been exposed to has led to the development of a system of higher education that is stratified by race, with racially minoritized institutions (e.g., HBCUs, HSIs, Tribal Colleges) mostly situated at the bottom of the hierarchy. As noted by Astin (2016), the stratified hierarchy of the postsecondary educational field is essentially maintained by reputational rankings, selectivity, and retention or degree completion rates (which are indirectly related to selectivity). This stratification is also racialized, as racially white institutions are more likely to be ranked higher, be more selective, and produce higher retention and degree completion rates. Inversely, HSIs are more likely to be broad-access, less-selective, under-resourced institutions that offer minimal bachelor's degree programs and with very few classified as research institutions (Núñez & Elizondo, 2012, 2015; Ortega et al., 2015; Santiago, 2006). As seen in chapter 2, the three HSIs highlighted in this book fit this profile in various ways.

Racialized Identities

A final consideration worth noting is that the racialized organizational identities of HSIs are connected to the individual racial identities of the students they enroll. By this I mean that as enrollment-driven institutions, HSIs are racially minoritized because they enroll racially minoritized students. An organizational identity, as proposed by Albert and Whetten (1985), is a socially constructed concept based on individual members' responses to the question, "Who are we as an organization?" In my own work I have found that this question is often connected to the enrollment of racially minoritized students (Garcia, 2013a, 2016). As such, the answer typically is, "We are a diverse institution." While HSIs are many other things, with varying levels of institutional-level diversity (e.g., control, type, size, Carnegie classification), the people within these institutions often make sense of an HSI organizational by stating the seemingly obvious (to them at least) that they enroll racially minoritized students (more often called diverse students) and often students in other minoritized groups based on income, citizenship, and language (which is why the term *diverse students* seems most appropriate to members). The response to this question also varies by racial group, with Latinx-identified people having a seemingly critical, more visceral response to the HSI identity than white students and non-Latinx students of color (Garcia & Dwyer, 2018).

In chapter 5, we saw that when members at RPU construct an HSI organizational identity, they do so from a race-neutral perspective. By this I mean that they contend to treat all students the same, regardless of racial background and with little regard for the racialization process that has subjugated some students throughout their educational histories. An important consideration is that 80% of the participants in the RPU non-student sample are white, which may be the reason for this race-neutral perspective, suggesting that the racial identity of the participants in a study does in fact affect how they construct a racialized identity. While there are processes that RPU enacts that other institutions can learn from, I continue to stress the importance of HSIs centering the experiences of racially minoritized people. I ask readers to consider whether it is acceptable for an organization that enrolls a large percentage of racially minoritized students to operate from a race-neutral perspective. Arguably no, as I have proposed that HSIs *must* work toward recognizing the racialized sociohistorical past of their organizational members and that they *must* work toward breaking down the structures that reinforce white supremacy and colonization (Garcia, 2017). Because of the isomorphic forces of the postsecondary educational field and the legitimization process that colleges and universities are exposed to, it seems acceptable to be Latinx-producing. In other words, scholars, legislators, parents, and regulatory bodies are not likely to criticize an institution that produces legitimized, and even more importantly, equitable outcomes for Latinx students, because white legitimized outcomes are acceptable within a field that reinforces white supremacy and values white normative standards. Until the field as a whole is willing to challenge these values, the racial stratification of institutions will remain intact. While I have started to explore the connections between individual racial identities and organizational racialized identities, (Garcia & Dwyer, 2018), more research needs to be done in order to understand this connection.

Reframing Policy Affecting HSIs

With this book, I call for reframing, or perhaps reaffirming, federal policy that supports HSIs. These institutions must remain a national priority, as they enroll the fastest-growing racially minoritized populations in the United States, including Latinxs, Asian Americans, and mixed-race people (Colby & Ortman, 2014; Núñez & Bowers, 2011). By 2060, it is projected that these three racial populations will represent 45% of the total US population (Colby & Ortman, 2014), making HSIs some of the most significant institutions within the postsecondary landscape.

Not only are HSIs (and other Minority-Serving Institutions) being charged with providing access to postsecondary education for the masses, with this book I am urging them to provide a culturally relevant, socially just education for these students; to prepare them for the job market; to provide them with financial aid and support; and to ensure that they graduate in a timely manner. In doing so, I argue that HSIs have the ability to transform the lives of not only individual racially minoritized students, but also their families, their communities, and the nation as a whole. This should not be taken lightly, as Latinxs and other racially minoritized groups are entering the job market at high rates and will need a postsecondary education that will support the nation's demand for a skilled work force. Latinxs continue to be employed in low-skill jobs and jobs that do not require bachelor's degrees, which is contributing to the persistent wage gap between Latinxs and whites (Carnevale & Fasules, 2017).

Expecting HSIs to provide outcomes for populations that continue to experience inequities in their educational and career trajectories, with little to no support from the federal government, is egregious. I cannot stress to legislators and policy advocates enough the importance of continuing to support both HSIs and the students who enroll in HSIs. This support must be financial, but it must also be symbolic. By symbolic I mean that the federal government must take responsibility for the sociohistorical mistreatment of Latinxs—a racially minoritized group that has been colonized, enslaved, and subjugated by the federal government for centuries, dating back to such events as the 1848 signing of the Treaty of Guadalupe Hidalgo, the 1898 signing of the Treaty of Paris, and the twentieth-century Cuban Revolution, which are just a few examples of the ways in which the US government has colonized the indigenous peoples of territories formerly ruled by Spain. In colonizing Latinx people—perhaps more appropriately labeled "Raza"—the federal government has continually stripped Latinxs of their language, culture, and educational rights, leading to drastic inequities in educational outcomes for this group (Garcia, 2018a). The symbolic recognition of HSIs, therefore, comes with the federal recognition of HSIs. By this I mean that policies that recognize and affirm HSIs are necessary as a way to acknowledge the sociohistorical racialization process that has kept Latinx students and HSIs on the margins. In this section I offer recommendations for enhancing current policies that move beyond symbolic support and into substantial provisions that will help HSIs better serve their student populations.

Recommit to Funding Pell Grants and Providing Financial Aid

The federal government must provide financial support in the form of direct aid to students who are likely to enroll in HSIs and in the form of federal research dollars directly to HSIs. In chapter 2, I provided an overview of the three institutions profiled in the counterstories. In reviewing IPEDS data, I found that the number of students who receive Pell Grants at these institutions is high, with 60% of all ACU students, 82% of all APC students, and 60% of all RPU students receiving Pell Grants. This high percentage of low-income Pell Grant recipients is not uncommon, as it has been well documented that students who attend HSIs are likely to be low-income Pell Grant recipients (Malcom-Piqueux & Lee Jr., 2011; Núñez & Bowers, 2011). On average, 50% of all Latinx undergraduate students receive Pell Grants, which is high compared to 34% of all white students (Excelencia in Education, 2017d). Moreover, in comparing the percentage of Latinx students receiving Pell Grants at the three institutions in this study to the national average of Latinx students receiving aid at all institutions, the financial need of students attending HSIs appears to be higher. As such, this is an opportunity to urge the federal government to continue supporting low-income students with the Pell Grant and other financial aid programs, with an emphasis on grants, not loans (Excelencia in Education, 2017d).

The HSIs that these low-income, Pell Grant students enroll in also benefit, albeit indirectly, which is particularly important for public HSIs that might not have the institutional capacity to financially support Latinx students. This is clear in looking at the data for the three institutions in this study, as ACU, a public, state-funded institution, provides a much lower level of institutional aid to students (less than 20% of students receive institutional aid) than APC or RPU, which are both private institutions and provide aid to more than 70% of all students. These data highlight the need for the federal government to consider how institutional need varies by control, with public HSIs potentially having a higher need for supportive legislation. This is one way that policy may be reframed, with the goal of better supporting public HSIs. In chapter 5, I highlighted how RPU is able to provide students with diverse financial aid packages, which contributes to their persistence and time to degree. Yet I remind the reader that RPU has the ability to offer institutional aid to students because it is a private institution.

Recommit to Funding Capacity-Building Grants for HSIs

The federal government must also (re)commit to providing direct funding to HSIs. This is especially important as research has proven that institutional expenditures are correlated with persistence and graduation, especially at institutions where there is a high number of Pell Grant recipients and other minoritized students with high need (Ehrenberg & Webber, 2010; Webber & Ehrenberg, 2010). Capacity-building grants are essential, as they feed directly into institutional expenditure budgets and are intended to enhance services and support. While the number of HSIs continues to increase annually, as does the annual Department of Education's Title V funding, data suggest that the funding has not kept pace, resulting in greater competition for these federal dollars (Santiago et al., 2016). As such, only about half of all HSIs (247 in fall 2014) have received federal funding to build capacity for serving students (Santiago et al., 2016). The competition for these funds is going to increase as the number of HSIs grows, unless there is larger commitment from the federal government. I call on legislators and policy advocates to consider several ways to reframe policy around capacity-building grants.

The most obvious consideration is that the budget for federal funding must increase every year in order to match the growth in the number of HSIs. However, simply increasing Title V funding, as the case has been (Santiago et al., 2016), is not enough when considering the rapid growth in the number of HSIs each year. The number of emerging HSIs is a good indicator that the HSI population will steadily increase each year (Excelencia in Education, 2017a). The federal government must take this into consideration as it develops and approves both Title V and Title III budgets specifically for capacity building within these institutions.

Second, I encourage other agencies, beyond the Department of Education, to reconsider their commitment to HSIs, including the Department of Agriculture, the Department of Housing and Urban Development, the Department of Defense, and the National Science Foundation. While the USDA continues to fund a number of HSI programs and HSI capacity grants, other agencies have wavered in their support over the past twenty years. In failing to support HSIs, federal agencies are missing an opportunity to contribute to the training and education of their future work force. Although federal funding for HSIs comes in the form of grants that represent a small portion of a college or university's operating budget, the funding has proven to be significant to HSIs (Santiago et al., 2016). Federal agencies must remember that HSIs are some of the most under-resourced institutions (Ortega et al., 2015), yet they enroll the future population of federal employees. Federal support is necessary to support the training and development of this population.

Like Flores and Park (2015), I believe strongly that when faculty and administrators take the initiative to submit applications for federal capacity-building grants, like those that are available to HSIs, this suggests a level of commitment to being an HSI and to serving Latinx and other minoritized students. In chapter 3, I only briefly mentioned the federal grants that ACU has obtained; through the data collection process, I found that ACU has been awarded multiple Department of Education Title V, A and B, grants as well as Title III funding. Moreover, ACU has worked directly with other federal agencies to ensure grant support, including the USDA. With these grants, ACU has established support services for students and developed faculty training programs, all with the goal of better serving Latinx and other minoritized students. As such, ACU's grant-getting activities have supported its ability to enact an identity for enhancing the experiences and racial/ethnic identities of Latinx students. Institutions like ACU are relying on the federal government's commitment to them.

In a previous study, I found that an HSI organizational identity is closely connected to HSI grants and the activities that are developed as a result of grant funding (Garcia, 2013a). I found that organizational members who make the most meaning of an HSI organizational identity are those who either are the principal investigators on the grants or are among the faculty and staff responsible for implementing the grants (Garcia, 2013a). Arguably, grants have the ability to change how organizational members' make meaning of their HSI organizational identity (Garcia, 2013a). The federal grants that are available to HSIs are also awarded based on an institution's commitment to addressing and decreasing the disparities in legitimized outcomes for Latinx students. Thus, there is a need to continue funding HSI programs through various federal agencies, as these programs not only enhance an HSI's meaning making around its organizational identity for serving Latinx students, but they also provide institutions with the necessary funding to address both legitimized and cultural outcomes for students. What can be learned from ACU is the extent to which federally funded grants can contribute to the development of a Latinx-enhancing identity.

Finally, with regard to the federal government's support, I call on legislators to consider the institutional diversity of HSIs and the impact this may have on their ability to be competitive in a grant competition. In particular, as the number of HSIs classified as high research institutions increases, the stratification of HSIs will also become enhanced, with high research universities potentially having a greater ability to compete for federal grants. This must be taken into consideration so that the distribution of federal resources remains equitable and institutions get the support they need with consideration of their institutional characteristics and strengths.

Reframing Requests for Proposals

The counterstories in chapters 3–5 also provide ideas for the requests for proposals (RFPs) that the federal government releases to HSIs. First, agencies can learn from the six considerations I offered earlier in this chapter. For example, I stressed the importance of HSIs developing curricular and programmatic offerings that are grounded in justice and liberation. Federal agencies must find ways to encourage HSIs to engage in the type of work that transforms curricula and practices. Although the federal government does not dictate curricula, it can provide the resources necessary for institutions to enhance their capacity to be more socially justice and liberating. I cannot stress enough the correlation between federal grants and the priorities of the federal government, which means federal agencies have the ability to make changes to their guidelines that will dictate changes in the ways institutions address their capacity for serving Latinx students.

I also argue that HSIs must hire faculty, staff, and administrators dedicated to justice and liberation, with an emphasis on eliminating the disparities between the compositional diversity of the student population at HSIs and that of the faculty, staff, and administrators. The federal government also has the ability to have an influence on hiring practices in HSIs. Federal agencies can dictate activities that would address the disparities in compositional diversity of faculty, staff, and administrators. Rather than calling for institutions to focus solely on legitimized outcomes, the federal government and the individual agencies that develop RFPs can place more value on such outcomes as increasing the number of Latinx tenure-track hires and high-level administrators over the life of multi-year grants. Although it seems like small progress, hiring even just two diverse tenure-track faculty members or high-level administrators in one year is not only quantifiable, but can have significant long-term effects on the outcomes produced by HSIs.

In addition to decreasing disparities in the compositional diversity of all constituents, hiring more diverse faculty, staff, and administrators can contribute to the development of the overall HSI organizational identity, as racially minoritized groups bring with them their own ways of knowing, being, teaching, and leading. In previous studies, I have found that the racial identities of organizational members are essential not only to the meaning making around an HSI organizational identity (Garcia & Dwyer, 2018), but also to the development of culturally relevant curricula and educational practices (Garcia, 2013a); however, HSIs must be proactive in recruiting, retaining, and promoting faculty, staff, and administrators of color, and the federal government must encourage this.

RFPs from the federal government that call for a focus on increasing the compositional diversity of faculty, staff, and administrators can have a significant effect on this seemingly slow-moving process. Institutions may need additional incentives to develop programs and policies that focus on the intentional recruitment, retention, and promotion of people of color. Moreover, the federal government has the ability to enforce Equal Employment Opportunity Commission (EEOC) hiring and prevent discrimination, and it should strongly consider its role in this. As institutions that depend on resources from the federal government, HSIs are more likely to respond to policy pressures set at the national level.

The counterstory in chapter 5 showed that high-touch practices such as advising and experiential learning are also essential to graduating students and assisting them with job placement upon graduation. Although a quarter of all Title V grants support the development of student support services (Santiago et al., 2016), more attention seems to be paid to developing services that support students academically while in college, rather than focusing on postgraduation career development.[1] I encourage federal agencies to consider postgraduation outcomes and career development a priority in RFPs, asking HSIs to be more intentional about their efforts to enhance the earning potential of their students. Although there is a need for more policy analysis of postgraduation outcomes, recent research suggests that Latinxs who graduate from HSIs have similar earnings as those who graduate from non-HSIs (Park, Flores, & Ryan Jr., 2017, 2018). This is an important finding, yet I wonder what their earnings would be if there were more attention paid to career development and outcomes at HSIs. Reports also suggest that spending more on instruction is correlated with higher salaries and the probability of full-time employment after graduation, especially for minoritized populations (Griffith & Rask, 2015). Future RFPs that call for an increased focus on enhancing postgraduation career outcomes and salaries, therefore, must focus on in-class instruction, like the experiential learning at RPU, as well as out-of-class support.

Final Thoughts: Moving From "Serving" to "Justice & Liberation"

The growth since the early 1990s in the number of Latinx college students and the HSIs that enroll them has complicated how we as researchers, practitioners, and legislators understand the experiences and outcomes of Latinx college students and the role that HSIs play in this. There has never been more of a need to understand how minoritized students experience college within compositionally diverse spaces. HSIs provide the perfect setting for this type of research. Moreover, there is a dire need to better understand these institutions as unique institutional forms, particularly as they are tasked with educating the fastest growing populations in the United States—populations that, as I regularly remind readers, have been historically oppressed in the educational system. While institutions of higher education were not designed for Latinx students (or any minoritized populations), I believe we have reached a moment in time when we can disrupt the historical legacy of exclusion and move toward a model of inclusion, or what I have otherwise called a decolonized institution (Garcia, 2018a).

If the goal is to liberate Latinx students and other minoritized populations, we must extend what is known about how HSIs serve racially minoritized individuals, while recognizing that they are subject to the ill nature of racism and white supremacy in the United States. We must first decolonize our own minds before we can decolonize HSIs, acknowledging that when we criticize racially minoritized institutions, we are buying into our own colonized mentality about how racially minoritized things can and should act within a society that is stratified by race. HSIs may very well be the best-equipped institutions for providing a culturally engaging space for Latinx and other minoritized students, leading to a greater sense of belonging and ultimately a greater level of persistence, graduation, and postgraduation career outcomes. Thus, there is a need for anti-deficit research, policy, and practices that center HSIs and the assets that they offer the field of higher education. With this book, I stress that we (scholars, practitioners, and legislators) must understand and acknowledge the racialization process that organizations, like individuals, are susceptible to before we can fully liberate HSIs. It also helps to understand that the US postsecondary system is stratified by race, which ultimately affects whether or not we will ever fully appreciate HSIs and the people within them. My hope is that readers will feel inspired by this text and the counterstories I've told and that they will feel better equipped to liberate HSIs and the minoritized populations within them. It's time to fight with and for HSIs.

Introduction: What It Means to Serve Students

1. I use the term *Latinx* as a gender-inclusive term for people who identify as having racial and ethnic roots in Mexico, Central and South America, and the Caribbean. The *x* replaces the *o* that is typically used to indicate inclusivity in the Spanish language.

2. In the original publication I used the term *Latinx-blind*; however, throughout this book I use the term *neutral* rather than *blind* in order to disrupt my own use of ableist language. This includes replacing the word *raceblind* with *race neutral*, despite the cited authors' use of the term.

Chapter One: Creating the Dominant Narrative

1. I use a lowercase *w* when referencing the white racial group as a way to decenter whiteness in my writing and research. I capitalize all other racial/ethnic groups as a way to center racially minoritized groups.

2. In this paragraph I use the term *kids* rather than *students* to reflect the language used by urban education scholars who have developed a body of literature around racial inequalities at the primary and secondary levels.

3. I use the term *minoritized* as a way to recognize that larger social contexts shape the experiences and outcomes of people from nondominant groups in the United States. Minoritized groups include racial, ethnic, gender, queer, socioeconomic, religious, and immigrant groups that have the least access to resources based on their social positioning.

4. For a list of the most and least diverse institutions, see Priceonomics Data Studio, "Ranking the most (and least) diverse colleges in America," Priceonomics, July 12, 2016, https://priceonomics.com/ranking-the-most-and-least-diverse -colleges-in/.

5. In this section I have intentionally chosen not to cite scholars who have published these criticisms, as I respect them and the important scholarship they have published. My comments are connected to a larger argument about the racialization of the entire system of higher education and how we all buy into it.

Chapter Two: White Institutions Becoming HSIs

1. I use the term *post-traditional* instead of *nontraditional* to imply that older, returning, part-time, and first-generation students, as well as students who are not college ready, are now more common, especially within HSIs. See Santiago (2013) for more details.

Chapter Three: Enhancing the Cultural Experience of Latinx Students

1. For regular updates on best practices, see Excelencia in Education's Growing What Works Database, http://www.edexcelencia.org/growing-what -works.

2. Names used in this narrative are pseudonyms, either chosen by the participant or assigned for anonymity.

3. The term *pocha* is slang, used by some Mexicans to refer to a non-Spanish-speaking (and often US-born) Mexican; the term may be considered derogatory.

4. For example, ESCALA Educational Services, Inc., is an organization dedicated to training faculty at HSIs how to be culturally competent, often working with institutions that have received federal HSI grants. See http://www .escalaeducation.com.

5. I use the gender-neutral pronouns of *their*, *them*, and *they* to avoid misgendering people based on their appearance.

6. Here the term *Latino* is used, rather than *Latinx*, to illustrate that not all people use *Latinx*. This professor did not use the term *Latinx* in their interview, therefore I do not use it in the narrative

Chapter Five: Pushing the Bar on Legitimized Outcomes

1. P-20 is used to reference the seamless pre-kindergarten through graduate school pipeline.

2. Here, I intentionally utilize the gender-neutral pronouns *them* and *they* because I do not know the gender of the student in Lisa's office.

Chapter Six: Reframing the HSI Narrative

1. For more details, see http://www.edexcelencia.org/growing-what-works.

AASCU Government Relations. (2017). *Top 10 higher education state policy issues for 2017*. Retrieved from http://www.aascu.org/policy/publications /policy-matters/Top10Issues2017.pdf.

Albert, S., & Whetten, D. A. (1985). Organizational identity. In L. L. Cummings & B. M. Staw (Eds.), *Research in organizational behavior* (vol. 7, pp. 263–295). Greenwich, CT: JAI Press.

Alemán, E., Jr. (2007). Situating Texas school finance policy in a CRT framework: How "substantially equal" yields racial inequity. *Education Administration Quarterly*, 43(5), 525–558. doi:10.1177/0013161X07303276.

Allen, W. R., & Jewel, J. O. (2002). A backward glance forward: Past, present, and future perspectives on Historically Black Colleges and Universities. *Review of Higher Education*, 25(3), 241–261.

Allen, W. R., Suh, S. A., González, G., & Yang, J. (2008). Qui bono? Explaining— or defending—winners and losers in the competition for educational achieve- ment. In T. Zuberi & E. Bonilla-Silva (Eds.), *White logic, white methods: Racism and methodology* (pp. 217–237). Lanham, MD: Rowman & Littlefield.

Alliance of Hispanic-Serving Institution Educators. (2017). AHSIE Home. Retrieved from https://www.ahsie.org/.

Alon, S. (2007). The influence of financial aid in leveling group differences in graduating from elite institutions. *Economics of Education Review*, 26, 296–311.

Alon, S., & Tienda, M. (2005). Assessing the "mismatch" hypothesis: Differ- ences in college graduation rates by institutional selectivity. *Sociology of Education*, 78, 294–315.

American Council on Education. (2017). Advocacy. Retrieved from http://www .acenet.edu/advocacy/Pages/default.aspx.

Anderson, J. D. (1988). *The education of Blacks in the south, 1860–1935*. Chapel Hill: University of North Carolina.

Andrew, M. (2017). Effectively maintained inequality in U.S. postsecondary progress: The importance of institutional reach. *American Behavioral Scientist*, 61(1), 30–48. doi:10.1177/0002764216682809.

Anzaldúa, G. (1987). *Borderlands/la frontera: The new mestiza*. San Francisco: Aunt Lute Books.

Arbelo-Marrero, F., & Milacci, F. (2016). A phenomenological investigation of the academic persistence of undergraduate Hispanic nontraditional students at Hispanic Serving Institutions. *Journal of Hispanic Higher Education*, 15(1), 22–40. doi:10.1177/1538192715584192.

Artze-Vega, I., Doud, E. I., & Torres, B. (2007). Más allá del inglés: A bilingual approach to college compositon. In C. Kirklighter, D. Cárdenas, & S. W. Murphy (Eds.), *Teaching writing with Latina/o students: Lessons learned at Hispanic-Serving Institutions* (pp. 99–117). Albany: State University of New York Press.

Association of Public and Land-grant Universities. (2017). Policy & Advocacy. Retrieved from http://www.aplu.org/policy-and-advocacy/.

Astin, A. W. (2016). *Are you smart enough? How colleges' obsession with smartness shortchanges students*. Sterling, VA: Stylus.

Astin, A. W., & Oseguera, L. (2004). The declining "equity" of American higher education. *Review of Higher Education*, 27(3), 321–341. doi:10.1353/rhe .2004.0001.

Aud, S., Fox, M. A., & KewalRamani, A. (2010). *Status and trends in the education of racial and ethnic groups (NCES 2010-015)*. Washington, DC: US Department of Education, National Center for Education Statistics.

Bastedo, M. N., & Bowman, N. A. (2010). U.S. News & World Report college rankings: Model institutional effects on organizational reputation. *American Journal of Education, 116*, 163–181.

Bastedo, M. N., & Bowman, N. A. (2011). College rankings as an interorganizational dependency: Establishing the foundation for strategic and institutional accounts. *Research in Higher Education, 52*(1), 3–23.

Bastedo, M. N., & Gumport, P. J. (2003). Access to what? Mission differentiation and academic stratification in U.S. public higher education. *Higher Education, 46*(3), 341–359.

Bensimon, E. M., & Malcom, L. (2012). *Confronting equity issues on campus: Implementing the equity scorecard in theory and practice*. Sterling, VA: Stylus.

Bess, J. L., & Dee, J. R. (2008). *Understanding college and university organizations: Theories for effective policy and practice* (vol. 1–2). Sterling, VA: Stylus.

Birnbaum, R. (1983). *Maintaining diversity in higher education*. San Francisco: Jossey-Bass.

Bonilla-Silva, E. (2014). *Racism without racists: Color-blind racism and the persistence of racial inequality in America* (4th ed.). Lanham, MD: Rowman & Littlefield.

Bonilla-Silva, E., & Zuberi, T. (2008). Toward a definition of white logic and white methods. In T. Zuberi & E. Bonilla-Silva (Eds.), *White logic, white methods: Racism and methodology* (pp. 3–27). Lanham, MD: Rowman & Littlefield.

Brown, A., & Lopez, M. H. (2013). *Mapping the Latino population, by state, county, and city*. Washington, DC: Pew Reseach Center.

Brown, M. C., II. (1999). Public black colleges and desegregation in the United States: A continuing dilemma. *Higher Education Policy, 12*(1), 15–25.

Brown v. Board of Education of Topeka, 347 U.S. 483 (1954).

Cabrera, N. L., Franklin, J. D., & Watson, J. S. (2017). *Whiteness in higher education: The invisible missing link in diversity and racial analyses*. Hoboken, NJ: Wiley.

Cabrera, N. L., Milem, J. F., Jaquette, O., & Marx, R. W. (2014). Missing the (student achievement) forest for all the (political) tress: Empiricism and the Mexican American controversy in Tucson. *American Education Research Journal, 51*(6), 1084–1118. doi:10.3102/0002831214553705.

Carnevale, A. P., & Fasules, M. L. (2017). *Latino education and economic progress: Running faster but still behind.* Washington, DC: Georgetown University: Center on Education and the Workforce.

Carnevale, A. P., & Strohl, J. (2013). *Separate and unequal: How higher education reinforces the intergenerational reproduction of white racial privilege.* Washington, DC: Georgetown University: Center on Education and the Workforce. Retrieved from https://cew.georgetown.edu/cew-reports/separate-unequal/.

Ceballo, R. (2004). From barrios to Yale: The role of parenting strategies in Latino families. *Hispanic Journal of Behavioral Sciences, 26*(2), 171–186.

Clark, B. R. (1970). *The distinctive college: Antioch, Reed, and Swarthmore.* Chicago: Aldine.

Colby, S. L., & Ortman, J. M. (2014). *Projections of the size and composition of the U.S. population: 2014 to 2060, Current Population Reports (P25-1143).* Washington, DC: US Census Bureau.

Cole, W. M. (2011). Minority politics and group-differentiated curricula at Minority-Serving Colleges. *Review of Higher Education, 34*(3), 381–422.

Contreras, F. E. (2005). The reconstruction of merit post-proposition 209. *Educational Policy, 19*(2), 371–395. doi:10.1177/0895904804274055.

Contreras, F. E., & Contreras, G. J. (2015). Raising the bar for Hispanic Serving Institutions: An analysis of college completion and success rates. *Journal of Hispanic Higher Education, 14*(2), 151–170. doi:10.1177/1538192715572892.

Contreras, F. E., Malcom, L. E., & Bensimon, E. M. (2008). Hispanic-Serving Institutions: Closeted identity and the production of equitable outcomes for Latino/a students. In M. Gasman, B. Baez, & C. S. V. Turner (Eds.), *Understanding Minority-Serving Institutions* (pp. 71–90). Albany: State University of New York Press.

Cuellar, M. (2014). The impact of Hispanic-Serving Institutions (HSIs), emerging HSIs, and non-HSIs on Latina/o academic self-concept. *Review of Higher Education, 37*(4), 499–530. doi:10.1353/rhe.2014.0032.

Cunningham, A., Park, E., & Engle, J. (2014). *Minority-Serving Institutions: Doing more with less.* Washington, DC: Institute for Higher Education Policy.

Darling-Hammond, L. (2010). Structured for failure: Race, resources, and student achievement. In H. R. Markus & P. M. L. Moya (Eds.), *Doing race: 21 essays for the 21st century* (pp. 295–321). New York: W. W. Norton & Company.

Dayton, B., Gonzalez-Vasquez, N., Martinez, C. R., & Plum, C. (2004). Hispanic-Serving Institutions through the eyes of students and administrators. *New Directions for Student Services, 105*, 29–40.

de los Santos, A. G. J., & Cuamea, K. M. (2010). Challenges facing Hispanic-Serving Institutions in the first decade of the 21st century. *Journal of Latinos and Education, 9*, 90–107.

DiMaggio, P. J., & Powell, W. W. (1983). The iron cage revisited: Institutional isomorphism and collective rationality in organizational fields. *American Sociological Review, 48*(2), 147–160.

Doran, E. E. (2015). Negotiating access and tier one aspirations: The historical evolution of a striving Hispanic-Serving Institution. *Journal of Hispanic Higher Education, 14*(4), 343–354. doi:10.1177/1538192715570638.

Dougherty, K. J., & Natow, R. S. (2015). *The politics of performance funding for higher education: Origins, discontinuations, and transformations.* Baltimore: Johns Hopkins University Press.

Dougherty, K. J., & Reddy, V. (2013). *Performance funding for higher education: What are the mechanisms? What are the impacts?* Hoboken, NJ: Wiley.

Easley, N. J., Bianco, M., & Leech, N. (2012). Ganas: A qualitative study examining Mexican heritage students' motivation to succeed in higher education. *Journal of Hispanic Higher Education, 11*(2), 164–178.

Ehrenberg, R. G., & Webber, D. A. (2010). Student service expenditures matter. *Change: The Magazine of Higher Learning, 42*(3), 36–39. doi:10.1080/00091381003704602.

Eisenhardt, K. M. (1989). Building theories from case study research. *Academy of Management Review, 14*(4), 532–550.

Espinosa, L. L., Crandall, J. R., & Tukibayeva, M. (2014). *Rankings, institutional behavior, and college and university choice: Framing the national dialogue on Obama's ratings plan.* Washington, DC: American Council on Education.

Espinoza, P. P., & Espinoza, C. C. (2012). Supporting the 7th-year undergraduate: Responsive leadership at a Hispanic-Serving Institution. *Journal of Cases in Educational Leadership, 15*(1), 32–50. doi:10.1177/1555458912440738.

Excelencia in Education. (2016a). *Emerging Hispanic-Serving Institutions (HSIs): 2014–2015.* Retrieved from http://www.edexcelencia.org/gateway/download/17266/1453981390.

Excelencia in Education. (2016b). *Emerging Hispanic-Serving Institutions (HSIs): 2014–2015.* Retrieved from http://www.edexcelencia.org/gateway/download/17265/1453981347.

Excelencia in Education. (2017a). Emerging Hispanic-Serving Institutions (HSIs): 2015–2016. Retrieved from http://www.edexcelencia.org/gateway/download/29690/1504618673.

Excelencia in Education. (2017b). Growing What Works. Database. Retrieved from http://www.edexcelencia.org/growing-what-works.

Excelencia in Education. (2017c). *Hispanic-Serving Institutions (HSIs): 2015–2016.* Retrieved from http://www.edexcelencia.org/gateway/download/29689/1504618448.

Excelencia in Education. (2017d). *Latinos in higher education and Pell grants.* Washington, DC: Excelencia in Education.

Fisher v. University of Texas, 570 U.S. (2013).

Fitts, S. (2009). Exploring third space in a dual-language setting: Opportunities and challenges. *Journal of Latinos and Education, 8*(2), 87–104. doi:10.1080/15348430902750668.

Flores, S. M., & Park, T. J. (2013). Race, ethnicity, and college success: Examining the continued significance of the Minority-Serving Institution. *Educational Researcher, 42*(3), 115–128. doi:10.3102/0013189x13478978.

Flores, S. M., & Park, T. J. (2015). The effect of enrolling in a Minority-Serving Institution for black and Hispanic students in Texas. *Research in Higher Education, 56*(3), 247–276. doi:10.1007/s11162-014-9342-y.

Fosnacht, K., & Nailos, J. N. (2015). Impact of the environment: How does attending a Hispanic-Serving Institution influence the engagement of baccalaureate-seeking Latina/o students? *Journal of Hispanic Higher Education, 15*(3), 187–204. doi:10.1177/1538192715597739.

Freeman, M. L. (2015). HEALing higher education: An innovative approach to preparing HSI leaders. In M. L. Freeman & M. Martinez (Eds.), *New Directions for Higher Education: Special Issue: College Completion for Latino/a Students: Institutional and System Approaches* (pp. 7–18). Hoboken, NJ: Wiley.

Gansemer-Topf, A. M., & Schuh, J. H. (2006). Institutional selectivity and institutional expenditures: Examining organizational factors that contribute to retention and graduation. *Research in Higher Education, 47*(6), 613–642.

Garces, L. M. (2015). The legal context and social science evidence in *Fisher v. University of Texas*. In U. M. Jayakumar & L. M. Garces (Eds.), *Affirmative action and racial equity: Considering the Fisher case to forge the path ahead* (pp. 3–20). New York: Routledge.

Garcia, G. A. (2013a). *Challenging the manufactured identity of Hispanic Serving Institutions: Co-constructing an organizational identity.* Unpublished dissertation, University of California, Los Angeles.

Garcia, G. A. (2013b). Does the percentage of Latinas/os affect graduation rates at four-year Hispanic Serving Institutions (HSIs), emerging HSIs, and non-HSIs? *Journal of Hispanic Higher Education, 12,* 256–268. doi:10.1177/1538192712467203.

Garcia, G. A. (2015). Using organizational theory to study Hispanic-Serving Institutions: An imperative research agenda. In A.-M. Núñez, S. Hurtado, & E. Calderón Galdeano (Eds.), *Hispanic-Serving Institutions: Advancing research and transformative practices* (pp. 82–98). New York: Routledge.

Garcia, G. A. (2016). Complicating a Latina/-o serving identity at a Hispanic Serving Institution. *Review of Higher Education, 40*(1), 117–143.

Garcia, G. A. (2017). Defined by outcomes or culture? Constructing an organizational identity for Hispanic-Serving Institutions. *American Education Research Journal, 54*(1S), 111S–134S. doi:10.3102/0002831216669779.

Garcia, G. A. (2018a). Decolonizing Hispanic-Serving Institutions: A framework for organizing. *Journal of Hispanic Higher Education, 17*(2), 132–147. doi:10.1177/1538192717734289.

Garcia, G. A. (2018b). What does it mean to be Latinx-serving? Testing the utility of the Typology of HSI Organizational Identities. *Association of Mexican American Educators Journal, 11*(3), 109–138. doi:http://dx.doi.org/10.24974/amae.11.3.363.

Garcia, G. A., & Dwyer, B. (2018). Exploring college students' identification with an organizational identity for serving Latinx students at a Hispanic Serving Institution (HSI) and emerging HSI. *American Journal of Education*, 124(2), 191–215.

Garcia, G. A., & Hudson, L. T. (2019). Exploring the (racialized) contexts that shaped the emergence of Hispanic Serving Institutions (HSIs) in Chicago: Implications for research and practice. In A. Hilton, B. Hinnant-Crawford, C. Newman, & S. Platt (Eds.), *Multicultural education in the 21st century: Innovative research and practices*. Charlotte, NC: Information Age.

Garcia, G. A., & Okhidoi, O. (2015). Culturally relevant practices that "serve" students at a Hispanic Serving Institution. *Innovative Higher Education*, 40(4), 345–357. doi:10.1007/s10755-015-9318-7.

Garcia, G. A., Patrón, O. E., Ramirez, J. J., & Hudson, L. T. (2018). Identity salience for Latino male collegians at Hispanic Serving Institutions (HSIs), emerging HSIs, and non-HSIs. *Journal of Hispanic Higher Education*, 17(3), 171–186. doi:10.1177/1538192716661907.

Garcia, G. A., & Ramirez, J. J. (2018). Institutional agents at a Hispanic-Serving Institution (HSI): Using social capital to empower students. *Urban Education*, 53(3), 355–381. doi:10.1177/0042085915623341.

Garcia, G. A., Ramirez, J. J., Patrón, O. E., & Cristobal, N. L. (forthcoming). *Constructing an HSI organizational identity at three Hispanic-Serving Institutions in the midwest: Ideal vs. current identity. Journal of Higher Education.*

Gasman, M., & Geiger, R. L. (2012). *Higher education for African Americans before the civil rights era, 1900–1964*. New York: Routledge.

Gasman, M., & Hilton, A. (2012). Mixed motivations, mixed results: A history of law, legislation, Historically Black Colleges and Universities, and interest convergence. *Teachers College Record*, 114(7), 1–34.

Gersick, C. J. G. (1991). Revolutionary change theories: A multilevel exploration of the punctured equilibrium paradigm. *Academy of Management Review*, 16(1), 10–36.

Gillborn, D. (2014). Racism as policy: A critical race analysis of education reforms in the United States and England. *Educational Forum*, 78(1), 26–41. doi:10.1080/00131725.2014.850982.

González, G. G. (2008). Segregation and the education of Mexican children, 1900–1940. In J. F. Moreno (Ed.), *The elusive quest for equality: 150 years of Chicano/Chicana education* (pp. 53–76). Cambridge, MA: Harvard Educational Review.

Gonzales, L. D. (2015). The horizon of possibilities: How HSI faculty can reshape the production and legitimization of knowledge within academia. In A.-M. Núñez, S. Hurtado, & E. Calderón Galdeano (Eds.), *Hispanic-Serving Institutions: Advancing research and transformative practices* (pp. 121–135). New York: Routledge.

González, R. G. (2008). College student civic development and engagement at a Hispanic Serving Institution. *Journal of Hispanic Higher Education*, 7(4), 287–300. doi:10.1177/1538192708320472.

Griffith, A. L., & Rask, K. N. (2015). The effect of institutional expenditures on employment outcomes and earnings. Retrieved from http://www.ilr.cornell.edu/sites/ilr.cornell.edu/files/cheri_wp167.pdf.

Guardia, J. R., & Evans, N. J. (2008). Factors influencing the ethnic identity development of Latino fraternity members at a Hispanic Serving Institution. *Journal of College Student Development, 49,* 163–181. doi:10.1353/csd.0.0011.

Gusa, D. L. (2010). White institutional presence: The impact of whiteness on campus climate. *Harvard Educational Review, 80*(4), 464–489.

Gutiérrez, K. (2008). Developing sociocritical literacy in the third space. *Reading Research Quarterly, 43*(2), 148–164. doi:10.1598/RRQ.43.2.3.

Gutiérrez, K., Baquedano-López, P., & Tejeda, C. (1999). Rethinking diversity: Hybridity and hybrid language practices in the third space. *Mind, Culture, and Activity, 6*(4), 286–303.

Gutiérrez, K., Rymes, B., & Larson, J. (1995). Script, counterscript, and underlife in the classroom: James Brown versus *Brown v. Board of Education. Harvard Educational Review, 65,* 445–471.

Hadi-Tabassum, S. (2006). *Language, space, and power: A critical look at bilingual education.* Buffalo, NY: Multilingual Matters.

Harmon, N. (2012). *The role of Minority-Serving Institutions in national college completion goals.* Washington, DC: Institute for Higher Education Policy.

Harper, S. R., Patton, L. D., & Wooden, O. S. (2009). Access and equity for African American students in higher education: A critical race historical analysis of policy efforts. *Journal of Higher Education, 80*(4), 389–413.

Harris, M. S. (2013). *Understanding institutional diversity in American higher education.* San Francisco: Wiley.

Heisserer, D. L., & Parette, P. (2002). Advising at-risk students in college and university settings. *College Student Journal, 36*(1), 69–83.

Hispanic Association of Colleges and Universities. (2017). 2017 HACU Legislative Agenda. Retrieved from https://www.hacu.net/images/hacu/govrel/2017LegislativeAgenda.pdf.

Hurtado, S., Alvarez, C. L., Guillermo-Wann, C., Cuellar, M., & Arellano, L. (2012). A model for diverse learning environments: The scholarship on creating and assessing conditions for student success. In J. C. Smart & M. B. Paulsen (Eds.), *Higher education: Handbook for theory and research* (pp. 41–122). New York: Springer.

Hurtado, S., & Carter, D. F. (1997). Effects of college transition and perceptions of the campus racial climate on Latino students' sense of belonging. *Sociology of Education, 70*(4), 324–345.

Hurtado, S., & Ponjuan, L. (2005). Latino educational outcomes and the campus climate. *Journal of Hispanic Higher Education, 4,* 235–251.

Institute for Higher Education Policy. (2009). *Impact of college rankings on institutional decision making: Four country case studies.* Washington, DC: Institute for Higher Education Policy.

Jayakumar, U. M., & Museus, S. D. (2012). Mapping the intersection of campus cultures and equitable outcomes among racially diverse student populations.

In S. D. Museus & U. M. Jayakumar (Eds.), *Creating campus cultures: Fostering success among racially diverse student populations* (pp. 1–27). New York: Routledge.

Jencks, C., & Riesman, D. (1968). *The academic revolution.* Garden City, NY: Doubleday Anchor.

Jones, T., Jones, S., Elliott, K. C., Russel Owens, L., Assalone, A. E., & Gándara, D. (2017). *Outcomes based funding and race in higher education: Can equity be bought?* London: Palgrave Macmillan.

Kerr, C. (1963). *The uses of the university.* Cambridge, MA: Harvard University Press.

Kiasatpour, S., & Lasley, S. (2008). Overcoming the challenges of teaching political science in the Hispanic-serving classroom: A survey of institutions of higher education in Texas. *Journal of Political Science Education, 4*(2), 151–168. doi:10.1080/15512160801998064.

Laden, B. V. (2001). Hispanic-Serving Institutions: Myths and realities. *Peabody Journal of Education, 76*(1), 73–92.

Laden, B. V. (2004). Hispanic-Serving Institutions: What are they? Where are they? *Community College Journal of Research and Practice, 28,* 181–198.

Ladson-Billings, G. (2006). From the achievement gap to the education debt: Understanding achievement in U.S. schools. *Educational Researcher, 35*(7), 3–12.

Lara, D., & Lara, A. (2012). From "Hell no!" to "¿Que pasó?": Interrogating a Hispanic-Serving Institution possibility. *Journal of Latinos and Education, 11*(3), 175–181. doi:10.1080/15348431.2012.686355.

Lopez, M. H., & Gonzalez-Barrera, A. (2013). *What is the future of Spanish in the United States?* Washington, DC: Pew Research Center.

MacDonald, V.-M. (2004). *Latino education in the United States: A narrated history from 1513–2000.* New York: Palgrave Macmillan.

MacDonald, V.-M., Botti, J. M., & Clark, L. H. (2007). From visibility to autonomy: Latinos and higher education in the U.S., 1965–2005. *Harvard Educational Review, 77*(4), 474–504.

Maestas, R., Vaquera, G. S., & Muñoz Zehr, L. (2007). Factors impacting sense of belonging at a Hispanic-Serving Institution. *Journal of Hispanic Higher Education, 6*(3), 237–256. doi:10.1177/1538192707302801.

Malcom-Piqueux, L., & Lee, J. M., Jr. (2011). Hispanic-Serving Institutions: Contributions and challenges. Retrieved from http://advocacy.collegeboard .org/sites/default/files/11b_4853_HSBC_PolicyBrief_WEB_120110.pdf.

Martin, J. (2002). *Organizational culture: Mapping the terrain.* Thousand Oaks, CA: Sage.

McCormick, A. C., & Zhao, C.-M. (2005). *Rethinking and reframing the Carnegie classification.* Palo Alto, CA: Carnegie Foundation for the Advancement of Teaching.

McDonough, P. M., Antonio, A. L., Walpole, M., & Perez, L. X. (1998). College rankings: Democratized college knowledge for whom? *Research in Higher Education, 39*(5), 513–537.

McGuire, M. D. (1995). Validity issues for reputational studies. In R. D. Walleri & M. K. Moss (Eds.), *New Directions for Institutional Research No. 88: Evaluating and Responsing to College Guidebooks and Rankings*. San Francisco: Jossey-Bass.

McLendon, M. K., Hearn, J. C., & Deaton, R. (2006). Called to account: Analyzing the origins and spread of state performance-accountability policies for higher education. *Educational Evaluation and Policy Analysis, 28*(1), 1–24.

Méndez Newman, B. (2007). Teaching writing at Hispanic-Serving Institutions. In C. Kirklighter, D. Cárdenas, & S. W. Murphy (Eds.), *Teaching writing with Latina/o students: Lessons learned at Hispanic-Serving Institutions* (pp. 17–35). Albany: State University of New York Press.

Meyer, A. D., Brooks, G. R., & Goes, J. B. (1990). Environmental jolts and industry revolutions: Organizational responses to discontinuous change. *Strategic Management Journal, 11*, 93–110.

Meyer, J. W., & Rowan, B. (1977). Institutionalized organizations: Formal structures as myth and ceremony. *American Journal of Sociology, 83*(2), 340–363.

Mills, C. W. (1997). *The racial contract*. Ithaca, NY: Cornell University Press.

Milner, I. H. R. (2012). Beyond a test score: Explaining opportunity gaps in educational practice. *Journal of Black Studies, 43*(6), 693–718. doi:10.1177/0021934712442539.

Moje, E. B., Ciechanowski, K. M., Kramer, K., Ellis, L., Carrillo, R., & Collazo, T. (2004). Working toward third space in content area literacy: An examination of everyday funds of knowledge and discourses. *Reading Research Quarterly, 39*(1), 38–70.

Mora, G. C. (2014). *Making Hispanics: How activists, bureaucrats, and media constructed a new American*. Chicago: University of Chicago Press.

Morphew, C. C. (2009). Conceptualizing change in the institutional diversity of U.S. colleges and universities. *Journal of Higher Education, 80*(3), 243–269. doi:10.1353/jhe.0.0047.

Moya, P. M. L., & Markus, H. R. (2010). Doing race: An introduction. In H. R. Markus & P. M. L. Moya (Eds.), *Doing race: 21 essays for the 21st century* (pp. 1–102). New York: W. W. Norton.

Muñoz, S. M., & Maldonado, M. M. (2011). Counterstories of college persistence by undocumented Mexicana students: Navigating race, class, gender, and legal status. *International Journal of Qualitative Studies in Education, 25*(3), 293–315. doi:10.1080/09518398.2010.529850.

Museus, S. D. (2014). The Culturally Engaging Campus Environments (CECE) model: A new theory of success among racially diverse college student populations. In M. B. Paulsen (Ed.), *Higher education: Handbook of theory and research* (vol. 29, pp. 189–227). New York: Springer.

Nasir, N. S. (2012). *Racialized identities: Race and achievement among African American youth*. Stanford, CA: Stanford University Press.

National Association of Independent Colleges and Universities. (2016). Policy & Advocacy. Retrieved from https://www.naicu.edu/policy-advocacy.

National Center for Education Statistics. (1980). *The condition of education for Hispanic Americans*. Washington, DC: US Department of Education.

National Center for Education Statistics. (2017). *The condition of education 2017 (NCES 2017-144)*. Washington, DC: US Department of Education.

Natividad, N. D. (2015). *Lucha Libre* and cultural icons: Identity formation for student success at HSIs. In M. L. Freeman & M. Martinez (Eds.), *New Directions for Higher Education: Special Issue: College Completion for Latino/a Students: Institutional and System Approaches* (pp. 91–101). Hoboken, NJ: Wiley.

Núñez, A.-M. (2014). *Counting what counts for Latinas/os and Hispanic-Serving Institutions: A federal ratings system and postsecondary access, affordability, and success*. Policy essay commissioned by the President's Advisory Commission on Educational Excellence for Hispanics, presented at the Postsecondary Access and Completion for All: Latinas/os in America's Future symposium, New York.

Núñez, A.-M. (2018). Flipping the HSI narrative: An HSI positionality. *Association of Mexican American Educators Journal*, 11(3), 276–295.

Núñez, A.-M., & Bowers, A. J. (2011). Exploring what leads high school students to enroll in Hispanic-Serving Institutions: A multilevel analysis. *American Educational Research Journal*, 48(6), 1286–1313. doi:10.3102/0002831211408061.

Núñez, A.-M., Crisp, G., & Elizondo, D. (2016). Mapping Hispanic-Serving Institutions: A typology of institutional diversity. *Journal of Higher Education*, 87(1), 55–83. doi:10.1353/jhe.2016.0001.

Núñez, A.-M., & Elizondo, D. (2012). *Hispanic-Serving Institutions in the U.S. mainland and Puerto Rico: Organizational characteristics, institutional financial context, and graduation outcomes*. White paper. San Antonio, TX: Hispanic Association of Colleges and Universities.

Núñez, A.-M., & Elizondo, D. (2015). Institutional diversity among four-year Hispanic-Serving Institutions. In A.-M. Núñez, S. Hurtado, & E. Calderón Galdeano (Eds.), *Hispanic-Serving Institutions: Advancing research and transformative practice* (pp. 65–81). New York: Routledge.

Núñez, A.-M., Murakami-Ramalho, E., & Cuero, K. K. (2010). Pedagogy for equity: Teaching in a Hispanic-Serving Institution. *Innovative Higher Education*, 35, 177–190. doi:10.1007/s10755-010-9139-7.

Obasogie, O. K. (2013). *Blinded by sight: Seeing race through the eyes of the blind*. Stanford, CA: Stanford University Press.

Olivas, M. (1982). Indian, Chicano, and Puerto Rican colleges: Status and issues. *Bilingual Review*, 9, 36–58.

Omi, M., & Winant, H. (2015). *Racial formation in the United States* (3rd ed.). New York: Routledge.

Ortega, N., Nellum, C., Frye, J., Kamimura, A., & Vidal-Rodriguez, A. (2015). Examining the financial resilience of Hispanic-Serving Institutions (HSIs) as they prepare the serve the next generation of Latino students. In A.-M. Nuñez, S. Hurtado, & E. Calderón Galdeano (Eds.), *Hispanic-Serving*

Institutions: Advancing research and transformative practice (pp. 155–176). New York: Routledge.

Park, T. J., Flores, S. M., & Ryan, C. J., Jr. (2017). *Labor market returns for graduates of Hispanic-Serving Institutions.* Paper presented at the National MSI Return on Investment Convening, Princeton, NJ.

Park, T. J., Flores, S. M., & Ryan, C. J., Jr. (2018). Labor market returns for graduates of Hispanic-Serving Institutions. *Research in Higher Education,* 59(1), 29–53. doi: 10.1007/s11162-017-9457-z.

Pedersen, J. S., & Dobbin, F. (2006). In search of identity and legitimation: Bridging organizational culture and neoinstitutionalism. *American Behavioral Scientist,* 49(7), 897–907. doi:10.1177/0002764205284798.

Posselt, J. R., Jaquette, O., Bielby, R., & Bastedo, M. N. (2012). Access without equity: Longitudinal analyses of institutional stratification by race and ethnicity, 1972–2004. *American Education Research Journal,* 49(6), 1074–1111. doi:10.3102/0002831212439456.

Ramírez-Dhoore, D., & Jones, R. (2007). Discovering a "proper pedagogy": The geography of writing at the University of Texas–Pan American. In C. Kirklighter, D. Cárdenas, & S. W. Murphy (Eds.), *Teaching writing with Latina/o students: Lessons learned at Hispanic-Serving Institutions* (pp. 63–86). Albany: State University of New York Press.

Regents of the University of California v. Bakke, 438 U.S. 265 (1978).

Rendon, L. I., Jalomo, R. E., & Nora, A. (2000). Theoretical considerations in the study of minority student retenion in higher education. In J. M. Braxton (Ed.), *Reworking the student departure puzzle* (pp. 127–156). Nashville, TN: Vanderbilt University Press.

Rodríguez, A., & Calderón Galdeano, E. (2015). Do Hispanic-Serving Institutions really underperform? Using propensity score matching to compare outcomes of Hispanic-Serving and non-Hispanic-Serving Institutions In A.-M. Núñez, S. Hurtado, & E. Calderón Galdeano (Eds.), *Hispanic-Serving Institutions: Advancing research and transformative practice* (pp. 196–217). New York: Routledge.

Rodríguez, A., & Kelly, A. P. (2014). *Access, affordability, and success: How do America's colleges fare and what could it mean for the president's rating plan?* Washington, DC: American Enterprise Institute.

Rodriguez, R. (2002). *Brown: The last discovery of America.* New York: Penguin.

Roebuck, J. B., & Murty, K. S. (1993). *Historically Black Colleges and Universities: Their place in American higher education.* Westport, CT: Praeger.

Rudolph, F. (1962). *The American college and university: A history.* New York: Vintage Books.

Ryan, J. F. (2004). The relationship between institutional expenditures and degree attainment at baccalaureate colleges. *Research in Higher Education,* 45(2), 97–114.

Santiago, D. A. (2006). *Inventing Hispanic-Serving Institutions (HSIs): The basics.* Washington, DC: Excelencia in Education.

Santiago, D. A. (2013). *Using a Latino lens to reimagine aid design and delivery.* Washington, DC: Excelencia in Education.

Santiago, D. A., Taylor, M., & Calderón Galdeano, E. (2016). *From capacity to success: HSIs, Title V, and Latino students*. Retrieved from http://www.edexcelencia.org/research/capacity.

Santos, J. L., & Acevedo-Gil, N. (2013). A report card of Latina/o leadership in California's public universities: A trend analysis of faculty, students, and executives in the CSU and UC systems. *Journal of Hispanic Higher Education, 12*(2), 174–200. doi:10.1177/1538192712470844.

Scott, M., Bailey, T., & Kienzi, G. (2006). Relative success? Determinants of college graduation rates in public and private colleges in the U.S. *Research in Higher Education, 47*(3), 249–279.

Scott, W. R. (1995). *Institutions and organizations*. Thousand Oaks, CA: Sage.

Sebanc, A. M., Hernandez, M. D., & Alvarado, M. (2009). Understanding, connection, and identification: Friendship features of bilingual Spanish–English speaking undergraduates *Journal of Adolescent Research, 24*, 194–217. doi:10.1177/0743558408329953.

Shor, I. (1992). *Empowering education: Critical teaching for social change*. Chicago: University of Chicago Press.

Smircich, L. (1983). Concepts of culture and organizational analysis. *Administrative Science Quarterly, 28*(3), 339–358.

Solórzano, D. G., & Yosso, T. J. (2002). Critical race methodology: Counter-storytelling as an analytical framework for education research. *Qualitative Inquiry, 8*(1), 23–44.

Stepler, R., & Lopez, M. H. (2016). *U.S. Latino population growth and dispersion has slowed since onset of the great recession*. Washington, DC: Pew Research Center.

Stevens, M. L. (2015). Introduction: The changing ecology of U.S. higher education. In M. W. Kirst & M. L. Stevens (Eds.), *Remaking college: The changing ecology of higher education*. Stanford, CA: Standford University Press.

Strayhorn, T. L. (2008). Sentido de pertenencia: A hierarchical analysis predicting sense of belonging among Latino college students. *Journal of Hispanic Higher Education, 7*(4), 301–320. doi:10.1177/1538192708320474.

Stuart, D. L. (1995). Reputational rankings: Background and development. In R. D. Walleri & M. K. Moss (Eds.), *New Directions for Institutional Research No. 88: Evaluating and Responding to College Guidebooks and Rankings* (pp. 13–20). San Francisco: Jossey-Bass.

Suddaby, R. (2010). Challenges for institutional theory. *Journal of Management Inquiry, 19*(1), 14–20. doi:10.1177/1056492609347564.

Suddaby, R. (2014). Can institutional theory be critical? *Journal of Management Inquiry, 24*(1), 93–95. doi:10.1177/1056492614545304.

Thelin, J. R. (2011). *A history of American higher education* (2nd ed.). Baltimore: Johns Hopkins University Press.

Tierney, W. G. (1988). Organizational culture in higher education: Defining the essentials. *Journal of Higher Education, 59*(1), 2–21.

Torres, V., & Zerquera, D. (2012). Hispanic-Serving Institutions: Patterns, predictions, and implications for informing policy discussions. *Journal of Hispanic Higher Education, 11*(3), 259–278. doi:10.1177/1538192712441371.

Turner, C. S. V., González, J. C., & Wood, J. L. (2008). Faculty of color in academe: What 20 years of literature tells us. *Journal of Diversity in Higher Education, 1*(3), 139–168. doi:10.1037/a0012837.

United States v. Fordice, 505 U.S. 717 (1992).

US Census Bureau. (2016). *FFF: Hispanic Heritage Month 2016.* Washington, DC: US Census Bureau.

US Department of Education. (2016). Programs: Developing Hispanic-Serving Institutions Program—Title V. Retrieved from https://www2.ed.gov/programs/idueshsi/awards.html.

Valdez, P. L. (2015). An overview of Hispanic-Serving Institutions' legislation: Legislation policy formation between 1979 and 1992. In J. P. Mendez, I. F. A. Bonner, J. Méndez-Negrete, & R. T. Palmer (Eds.), *Hispanic-Serving Institutions in American higher education: Their origin, and present and future challenges* (pp. 5–29). Sterling, VA: Stylus.

Vander Schee, B. A. (2007). Adding insight to intrusive advising and its effectiveness with students on probation. *NACADA Journal, 27*(2), 50–59.

Veysey, L. R. (1965). *The emergence of the American university.* Chicago: University of Chicago Press.

Wathington, H., Pretlow, J., & Barnett, E. (2016). A good start? The impact of Texas' developmental summer bridge program on student success. *Journal of Higher Education, 87*(2), 150–177.

Webber, D. A., & Ehrenberg, R. G. (2010). Do expenditures other than instructional expenditures affect graduation and persistence rates in American higher education? *Economics of Education Review, 29,* 947–958.

Weidman, J. C., Nelson, G. M., & Radzyminski, W. J. (1984). Books perceived to be basic reading for students of higher education. *Review of Higher Education, 7*(3), 279–287.

Welner, K. G., & Carter, P. L. (2013). Achievement gaps arise from opportunity gaps. In P. L. Carter & K. G. Welner (Eds.), *Closing the opportunity gap: What America musst do to give every child an even chance.* New York: Oxford University Press.

Whetten, D. A., & Mackey, A. (2002). A social actor conception of organizational identity and its implications for the study of organizational reputation. *Business Society, 41*(4), 393–414. doi:10.1177/0007650302238775.

Wilder, C. S. (2013). *Ebony and ivy: Race, slavery, and the troubled history of America's universities.* New York: Bloomsbury.

Wright, B. (1991). The "untameable savage spirit": American Indians in the colonial colleges. *Review of Higher Education, 14*(4), 429–452.

Yin, R. K. (2009). *Case study research: Design and methods* (4th ed.). Los Angeles, CA: Sage.

achievement gap: definition of, 9; opportunity gap and, 9, 22. *See also* opportunity gap; racialization

Adams State University. *See* Higher Education Administration and Leadership

Advancement Via Individual Determination (AVID), 106

Alcorn State University, 10

Alliance of Hispanic-Serving Institution Educators (AHSIE), 95

Amarillo Private College (APC): academic programs, 39; advocacy, 89; affordability, 82; bilingual program, 81; campuses, 38; career development, 87; community-based participatory research, 87; compositional diversity, 40; counterstory, 78; institutional characteristics of, 5, 37–38; mission, 37–38, 85; open-access, 38, 79–80; organizational identity of, 118; revenue, 38; student support programs, 40

American Association of State Colleges and Universities (AASCU), 94, 97

American Council on Education (ACE), 94, 98

Americans with Disabilities Act (ADA), 66

anti-deficit research, 137

anti-racism, 62

Arizona House Bill 2281, 22

Association for the Study of Higher Education (ASHE), 18

Association of Public and Land-grant Universities (APLU), 94, 98

Azul City University (ACU): academic programs, 34–35, 55; administration, 56; black and brown student tension at, 57; budget concerns, 59; campuses,

35, 54; compositional diversity, 36, 59; counterstory, 51–52; ENLACE, 55; faculty, 58, 134; grants, 37, 55; HSI designation, 55–57; inclusivity, 65–67; institutional characteristics of, 5, 33–34; Latinx support programs, 53–54, 134; mission, 33; organizational identity of, 116, 124; racism at, 65, 69; student housing, 56

bilingualism: 6, 35, 37–38, 118; bilingual institutions, 75–78, 119, 124

Birnbaum, Robert, 20

Brown v. Board of Education of Topeka, 11, 22

capacity-building grants, 132–33

Carnegie classification, 32, 129

Catholic colleges, 20

Cheyney University, 10

Civil Rights Act (1964), 22–23

Clark, Burton, 19

color-neutral, 114. *See also* race-neutral

counternarrative approach, 4, 26; critical race and, 5; policy implications of, 115

critical race methodology, 5, 22, 25, 26

Cuban Revolution, 131

cultural indicators of uniqueness, 124

cultural self, 90, 92

cultural theory, 28–30

decolonization, 62, 137

Deferred Action for Childhood Arrivals (DACA), 97

deficit-based perspective, 4

Department of Education College Cost Reduction and Access Act (CCRAA), 37

Developing Hispanic-Serving Institutions (program), 2
dominant racial narrative, 4, 6–7, 25–26, 51; population measures and, 92; on reframing, 116
DREAM Act, 60

environmental theory, 28–29
Educational Opportunity Program (EOP), 51
educational pipeline, 7, 9
Equal Employment Opportunity Commission (EEOC), 136
Excelencia in Education, 95

Fisher v. University of Texas, 23
Free Application for Federal Student Aid (FAFSA), 102

Gasman, Marybeth, 21
GEAR UP, 62
Geiger, Roger, 21
graduate students, 64, 88

Higher Education Act (HEA), 2, 7, 15, 98
Higher Education Administration and Leadership (HEAL) program, 50
Higher Learning Commission, 92
Hispanic Association of Colleges and Universities (HACU), 2, 7, 37, 41, 52, 56, 73; role of, 95, 98
Hispanic Higher Education Coalition (HHEC), 2, 7, 15
Hispanic-Serving Institutions (HSIs): comparative evaluation and, 46; criticism of, 45, 62; culture, 30; current HSI identity, 116; curricular offerings at, 11, 16, 50, 117, 135; definition of, 1; dominant narrative and, 26; emerging, 3, 25, 27, 133; federal designation, 1–2, 5, 7, 73; as federally constructed, 28; federally eligible, 125; federal recognition of, 15–16, 131; funding for, 16, 98, 132–34; geographic location of, 27; hiring practices at, 135; Hispanic-enrolling, 16, 27, 128; history of, 15, 121; ideal HSI identity, 31, 116; incentives, 136; institutional diversity and, 32, 117, 123, 134; legitimacy and, 29, 97, 122–23, 125; liberation-based model, 6, 117, 135, 137; Midwest HSI Study, 26–27, 32–33, 46; organizational identity, 1, 4, 60, 125, 127, 134–35; practical considerations for, 115, 133, 135; Puerto Rico, 1, 27; racial categories and, 15; rankings, 13–14; reframing and reaffirming of, 116, 121, 130–31; service learning at, 50; striving, 3; subjugation of, 25; symbolic recognition of, 131; undergraduate enrollment of, 2–3, 5, 25. *See also* racially minoritized institutions; *Typology of HSI Organizational Identities*
Historically Black Colleges and Universities (HBCUs): establishment of, 10, 19; outcomes-based funding policies at, 96. *See also* racially minoritized institutions

Illinois Board of Higher Education, 82
Illinois Monetary Award Program (MAP), 38, 82, 83, 102, 120
immigrants: importance of serving, 5; minority-serving institutions and, 63; as students of color, 24; tuition and, 60
institutional effectiveness: characteristics of, 128; diversity and, 20, 45, 74, 97; excellence and, 12; indicators of, 3, 47–48, 91; ranking system and, 17
institutional theory, 28, 30, 93–94; coercive isomorphism, 94, 96, 122; mimetic process, 95; normative pressures, 94
intersectionality, 67–68
IPEDS (Integrated Postsecondary Educational Data System) data, 5, 26, 33, 51, 131

Jencks, Christopher, 20

Kerr, Clark, 18

land-grant institutions, 10–11. *See also* Association of Public and Land-grant Universities

Latinx: commitment to serving, 133; community, 30, 50, 83, 130; definition of, 139n1; demographics, 72, 97; education gap of, 7, 49, 61, 69; equitable outcomes for, 113, 135; financial needs, 131; HSI enrollment threshold for, 5; indicators of serving, 3, 17, 31, 69, 118; neutral perspective of, 6, 99; postsecondary completion rates for, 72; racial ways of knowing, 5–6, 78, 83, 99; sense of belonging, 49; sociohistorical mistreatment of, 131; STEM degrees, 25; students as transformational tools, 83–84
Latinx-neutral perspective. *See* Latinx
Latinx organizational identities, 26, 31–32, 51; Latinx-enhancing, 5, 37, 49, 70, 124, 134; Latinx-producing, 6, 45, 99, 119, 129; Latinx-serving, 6, 41–42, 118, 124
Lincoln University, 10
linguistic identity, 74–75

majority Mexican American school districts, 22
mental illness, 93
Midwest Higher Learning Commission, 82, 92
minoritized groups: 139n2; access and outcomes for, 12, 73
Minority-Serving Institutions (MSIs), 11, 13, 51, 63, 130. *See also* racially minoritized institutions
Monetary Award Program (MAP). *See* Illinois Monetary Award Program
Morrill Act (1862, 1890), 10

National Association of Independent Colleges and Universities (NAICU), 94–95, 98
Native American Pacific Islander–Serving Institutions (AANAPISIs), 79
"Negro" colleges, 20
neoliberal education agenda, 64–65
Nevada State College Nepantla program, 51

"new accountability movement," 23–24
"new racism," 112; abstract liberalism and, 112; cultural racism, 113; minimization of racism, 114; naturalization and, 113

opportunity gap, 9, 22; inequitable funding models and, 22. *See also* achievement gap; racialization
oppression: history of, 7
organizational identity, 30, 92, 116. *See also* Hispanic-Serving Institutions; Latinx
outcomes-based funding models, 91; performance policies, 96

peer assessment, 14
Pell Grants, 82, 102, 120, 131–32
people of color: discrimination of, 23–24; economic outcomes for, 114; entry into postsecondary education, 33; organizational identity and, 70; promotion of, 136; recognition of, 111–12; representation of, 58–62, 68; sociohistorical contexts of, 18; university representation and, 9–10, 14, 58–59, 74
Plessy v. Ferguson, 22
population ecology theory, 20
postsecondary system: affordability, 93; desegregation of, 23; stratification of, 12, 45, 137; white racial dominance in, 23–24, 28
Protestant colleges, 20
punctuated equilibrium, 125–26

race-neutral: lens, 6, 111, 129, 139n2; organizational theories and, 121; postsecondary criticism and, 12, 22; research, 126
racialization: consequences of, 12–13, 23, 45; definition of, 7–8; educational inequities and, 9, 39, 122; faculty and, 58; framework, 4, 33; funding and, 22; hierarchy of, 9, 11, 13, 128; organizational theory and, 127; othering and, 8; process, 9, 13, 17–18, 25, 78

racialized knowledge, 21, 121; legitimacy and, 126, 128; ways of knowing, 135

racially minoritized institutions, 11–12, 16, 18; access for students of color, 23–24, 130; context and, 115; legitimacy and, 126–7; location of, 28; scholarship and, 21; stratification of, 13, 15, 17–18, 45; valuation of, 24–26, 29, 126, 128

"Raza," 131

Regents of the University of California v. Bakke, 23

requests for proposals (RFPs), 134–36

Riesman, David, 20

Rosado Private University (RPU): academic programs, 43, 108–10; advising, 103, 107–8, 119; campuses, 38; career development, 104, 108; cohort model, 103; compositional diversity, 44, 111; counterstory, 98; experiential learning, 105, 108–11, 120, 136; graduation rate, 101, 112; grants, 45, 104; institutional characteristics of, 42, 98; mission, 42; open-access, 38; organizational identity of, 119; revenue, 38; scholarships, 102–3; student support programs, 43–44

Rudolph, Frederick, 19

second-order change processes, 125, 126

segregation, 10

self-efficacy, 17

social constructionist perspective, 46, 127

student engagement, 17

student support programs: at ACU, 35; at APC, 40; at RPU, 43

third space, 76, 90–91, 118–19; definition of, 77–78; in organizational change, 126

Title III, 2, 133

Title V, 2, 37, 41, 45; competition for, 132–33; Developing HSIs program grants, 96, 136

Treaty of Guadalupe Hidalgo, 131

Treaty of Paris, 131

Tribal Colleges, 128. *See also* racially minoritized institutions

TRiO program, 35, 44, 61

Tucson Unified School District, 22

Tuskegee University, 10

Typology of HSI Organizational Identities, 5, 28, 31, 33, 121

undocumented students, 51, 53, 97; advising and, 103; centers for, 54; organizational identity and, 70; scholarships for, 60, 102

United States v. Fordice, 22

University of Maryland Eastern Shore, 10

University of Miami, 76

University of Texas at San Antonio (UTSA), 74

US Constitution, 8

Veysey, Lawrence, 19

ways of knowing. *See* racialized knowledge

whiteness: conceptualization of, 8, 139n1; normalization of, 9–11, 13, 21; policy narratives and, 24–25, 115; privileged identities and, 8; racial order and, 22

white normative standards, 3, 6, 16, 29, 39, 78; operation outside, 126

white supremacy, 22

Wilberforce University, 10

Wilder, Craig Steven, 21